To Amera

A Path Through

Nice to meet you!

Janra Olsen Spratt

A Path Through

Janna Olsen Spratt

Copyright © 2012 by Janna Olsen Spratt.

Library of Congress Control Number:		2012906954
ISBN:	Hardcover	978-1-4691-9847-7
	Softcover	978-1-4691-9846-0
	Ebook	978-1-4691-9848-4

To order additional copies of this book, contact:
Xlibris Corporation
1-888-795-4274
www.Xlibris.com
Orders@Xlibris.com
103200

Contents

Acknowledgments

To my mother, Eva Phillips Olsen, I owe a debt of gratitude for showing me by example how to walk with God through difficult circumstances.

To my children, Dwayne and Brenda, I owe a world of thanks for loving me and believing in me through the years.

To my late husband, Larry, I give the credit for being a 1 Peter 3:7 husband who loved me to wholeness.

Introduction

"Thus says the Lord, Who makes a way in the sea and a path in the mighty waters."

—Isaiah 43:16 (AMP)

In the pages of this book you will see my footprints in the sands of time as I make my way through life's triumphs and tragedies. My hope is that I have been able to convey the positive outcome and personal growth that resulted in spite of sometimes negative circumstances. Although chronological events are important and I have tried to remember them as they happened, the spiritual encounters were defining moments that shaped me, giving my life meaning that I would not have known otherwise.

I have written this as my testimony to the faithfulness of God throughout my life—from childhood to old age. The title *A Path Through* is meant to convey the idea of overcoming and going through circumstances to the other side, in victory. This is the legacy I wish to leave my children and grandchildren, that life happens, and you can go through anything with God as your companion and guide.

My intention is not to hurt anyone but to tell my story and how God brought me through to real freedom and to hope. Where my life intersects with others, I have tried to be honest about my feelings. The mistakes I made were not hidden or glossed over, but they were part of my learning and have made me the person I am today.

I pray that those who will read this book will find hope for whatever they are going through in their life. For explanations as to some of the terms used and events perhaps not understood, you will find appendices in the back of the book.

Chapter 1
The Waters Of Uncertainty

"When you pass through the waters,
I will be with you,"

—Isaiah 43:2 (AMP)

Little did I know as I packed my books in February that I would unpack them two months later. And as I prayed for the Lord to lead us to where we should go, I did not know that my husband, Larry, and I would not be going to the same place.

We were planning to move back to the Abbotsford, Langley, area in BC where we had lived some twelve years earlier. It all started with a conversation over lunch with Dwayne and Maureen, our son and our daughter-in-law. We were talking about seniors' housing being in short supply and that it might be a good idea for us to think about where we would like to live and putting our name into some places.

Our plan was to move back to the Coast into an apartment, and from there we could decide which seniors' housing would be the right place for us to make an application for. We needed to look for an apartment there, so we decided we would drive to Surrey to visit our son, Dustin, and his family, and from there we would search.

Larry would be eighty years old on March 4, and we could celebrate his birthday as well as look for a place at the same time. Our children

11

planned a big party with our family and friends. This was a milestone for Larry because his life had nearly been cut short a few times before this, and making it this far was somewhat of a miracle.

Someone has said, "If you want to make God laugh, tell Him your plans." We were praying about what we should do, and it seemed to us that this was a way to test the waters. We left Castlegar the morning of March 1. Our plan was to travel halfway, stay overnight at Princeton, and finish the trip the next day.

We would be traveling through mountain passes which could have snow on the highway, so we wanted to give ourselves lots of time. Larry was a truck driver with more than three million miles behind him, so he was not too concerned about driving.

Although there was quite a bit of snow in the first pass, we made good time, arriving in Princeton early in the afternoon. The next morning after breakfast, we set out for the final part of our trip. It was a beautiful, sunny day, and we felt good about the trip thus far.

There was quite a lot of snow on the Hope—Princeton highway, but Larry was not concerned. Our 2008 Toyota seemed to handle the road conditions well. When we passed the Hope turnoff and began the divided freeway with two lanes going each way, we felt we had it made. The worst was over!

We passed a semi and were still in the left lane when suddenly the left front wheel got caught in a deep pothole. Larry struggled desperately to keep the car on the road, but it seemed as if a force stronger than him wrenched the wheel out of his hands, and we were immediately airborne. I called out, "Lord, help us," as the car flew off the road into the median which was full of snow.

Everything happened so fast; it seemed as if we were watching a movie, spellbound. We sat there with our seat belts on while the car careened crazily down the embankment spinning around and doing donuts and other turns. As we spun around, there was a lot of snow going across the windshield. The back end of the car slammed into the snowbank as we fishtailed, and the trunk opened, spilling suitcases and some of the other contents.

As the car was spinning and slamming into banks, the big back window smashed in as well as the backside windows. The backseat was filled with snow. My glasses flew off and were later found in the snow in the backseat, and my left hearing aid flew out and was later found on the dash.

At one point we started to climb the bank toward the traffic on the eastbound side, but it was a steep incline, and we were kept from going there. For one second I saw it, I thought we might go into it; but instead the car rolled back, turned, and came to rest on its right side on two wheels leaning against a snow-covered bank. Larry had to brace himself with his feet in order not to fall down on me.

In the midst of all this turmoil, we sat there with our seat belts on. Strangely, we felt protected. The front window did not even have a crack in it, the front side windows were untouched, and the air bags did not deploy. We were not seriously injured.

I reached for my cell phone, began dialing 911, and then a man was standing there, peering in the front window asking if we were all right. We shouted we were OK. Just then two RCMP officers appeared. They were traveling by and saw what happened. One of them had been headed west, and the other one was headed east. Coincidence?

A truck driver had stopped and come to help as well as some other men. There were at least six men there. When we said we were all right, with us still in the car, they put the car back on four wheels. They opened the doors and helped us out of the car, asking again and again, "Are you sure you are all right?" We assured them we were a little shaken but otherwise all right.

We each had two men, one on each side, holding on to us as we trudged through the deep snow across the median and up the bank to the highway. We waited in the police car until the ambulance came. After the paramedics checked us out and the police took our statements, we were taken to the Fraser Canyon Hospital at Hope, BC, for further examination.

Besides being shaken up, Larry had some cuts on his hands and arms which they bandaged. The cuts were probably from the shattered glass when the back windows smashed. I had a black eye. I must have banged my head on the window frame, although I did not remember just when it happened.

Larry jokingly said that he never flew a Toyota before and that I should wear a sign that said, "My husband didn't do this to me." The X-ray on my neck showed no broken bones. In the emergency room, Larry was given a bed to rest on, but I was free to walk around.

One of the police officers followed us to the hospital and gave us a copy of the report as well as the address of the towing company that had taken care of our car. We called Maureen back in Castlegar to tell her what happened. Then we called our son, Dustin, in Surrey who came to the hospital.

While we were waiting for the hospital to release us, Dustin went to retrieve our belongings from the car. His remark after looking at the car and taking pictures was "Somebody was looking after you." We had been protected in the front seat. In fact the front of the car had almost no damage. There was a very small dint on the right front fender, but the front doors were not damaged.

Most of the damage was in the back, on the roof over the back window, and on the trunk. The tow truck driver said the frame was bent. The car was a write-off, but we walked away from it with only minor injuries. Although the accident happened about ten thirty in the morning we were not released from the hospital until 4:00 PM.

Three days later, about 2:00 AM, Larry woke me up saying that he was having trouble with his balance. He had gotten up to go to the bathroom and was having trouble walking. I went upstairs and called Dustin. He decided to take Larry to the emergency at the Delta Hospital. He was able to walk with help, so we took him in the car.

After some tests, the doctor there decided to admit him. He believed Larry had suffered a small stroke and wanted to keep him for observation. It was the day of Larry's birthday party. Because some people had traveled some distance to be there, it was decided to go ahead with the party.

That night the friends and family who were gathered together sang "Happy Birthday" to Larry in his hospital bed via someone's cell phone. The hospital allowed him to have visitors after hours, so some of the children went in to see him. He was glad to see them and seemed to be in good spirits, enjoying the attention.

With no further incidents the hospital discharged him on March 7. But it was not over yet. In the early morning hours of March 8, Larry woke me to tell me that he was having trouble with his legs again. I called Dustin, and he determined this time it was worse. He called an ambulance. He asked that they take him to Royal Columbian, a hospital specializing in cardiac care.

Within a short time he had suffered another stroke. This time he was paralyzed on his right side, and he could not speak. The MRI showed blockage in arteries that had not been checked in previous CT scans. He also had pneumonia. He was transferred to a private room which made it possible for family members to stay with him around the clock. He was never left alone even at night; someone was always there with him.

As his pain increased and he had more difficulty breathing, he was sedated more heavily. At first he responded to us by squeezing our hands but gradually that lessened then stopped altogether as the sedation became stronger and more frequent. We came together as a family, something Larry always prayed for. The decision was made that there would be no medical intervention to keep him alive with machines but to let him die with dignity.

Although Brenda D. (Larry's daughter) and I anointed him with oil and prayed for a miracle that he would be restored to health, it was not to be. On March 21 at approximately 4:00 AM, with his oldest daughter, Gayle, by his side, Larry was ushered into the presence of the Lord. He had reached his milestone of eighty years, and he was ready to go to his final home.

In one of his devotionals, Selwyn Hughes said, "There are treasures to be found in every period of darkness, even the darkness of shattered hopes and plans." We had started out with plans for a new chapter in our life together; now those dreams were shattered.

Chapter 2
Rivers Of Grief

"And through the rivers they shall not overwhelm You;"

—Isaiah 43:2 (AMP)

My devotional reading asks the question "Can you dare believe that in the period when important plans have broken up God is at work moving the scenery for the next act? The shattering of our plans is the prelude to the advancement of His plans. There is a point and a purpose to what has happened to you."

Dwayne, Laura-Lee, Elizabeth, and I went to the Valley View Memorial Gardens to make the arrangements for the cremation and burial. There are many different areas and types of burial sites, and when the lady helping us heard that Larry loved the outdoors she showed us Amble Lane. The upright markers of various sizes with cement walks and benches among trees seemed the perfect place.

On March 25, we buried the love of my life in Amble Lane with many friends and relatives attending. Because it was a cold spring morning the graveside service was short. Afterward a memorial lunch was held at Dustin and Laura-Lee's clubhouse. This was attended by family and friends mainly from the Lower Mainland. Three weeks after his eightieth birthday, he was gone; and now we, as a family, shared our memories as we spent time together.

16

I came home with Dwayne and Maureen. They offered for me to stay with them on the first night, but I needed to be alone to let the events of the last three weeks sink in. The beautiful big basement suite in their home was a haven to rest in. The last three weeks had been anything but restful. I was still trying to come to grips with all of the events that had unfolded so rapidly.

The words of a song that I had sung as a solo when I was much younger kept running through my mind. The title is "Submission," and it speaks about the path that brought me close to God being not a path that I would have chosen; but since it has been laid on me, I will bear it for the Master's sake. The chorus haunted me.

"Not what I wish to be, nor where I wish to go,
for who am I that I should choose my way?
The Lord shall choose for me, 'tis better far, I know.
So let Him bid me go or stay."

If there is a point and a purpose to everything that is happening in my life, then I need the leading of the Lord for the next act. I've been in quite a few different acts, and most of the time there's been no rehearsal. I've never been this way before. Where's my security, my safe place? I read somewhere, "Security is not the absence of danger but the presence of God in the midst of danger."

As I read and study the Word of God, I believe that my security is in a person, Jesus Christ. In John 14 Jesus said, "Let not your heart be troubled," and then, "Peace I leave with you. My peace I give to you. Let not your heart be troubled or fearful." So I ask the question, "Can I trust Jesus? Is He everything He says He is?" If it is true that you will never know if Jesus is real until you risk everything and follow Him, then I was about to find out for myself His reality.

We had a traditional memorial service in the church we've been attending in Castlegar. Our granddaughter, Ayron, read the eulogy which was about his life from being young on the farm to his adult trucking days. Maureen had phoned people who would not already know. Everything was looked after so well by our family.

Many people attended from the community which was a tribute to his love for the people whose lives he had touched. He loved people, and that love came through. He was always cheerful and optimistic seeing the good in others. This was expressed by many people who came to pay their respects.

Larry's health had deteriorated this last year, and the doctors had not been able to find the reason. The two CT scans he had did not reveal the blocked artery, only the last MRI showed the truth, but it was too late. The "why" questions surface. Why did the blockage never show up before? We had the answer to why he kept saying over and over again, "There's something wrong, I can feel it."

One of the most profound questions was "If God protected us *in* the accident, why had He not protected us *from* it happening at all?" Larry's brother, Glenn, told me that the reason I was still here was because God has something for me to do. If that is true then I need to discover the purpose for my life.

Before this time in my life I would pray about the plans I made and hope that God was leading, but now I was on a different path, that of discovering the purpose for my existence in the first place. I believe that God has the perfect plan for my life; it was in place before I was even born. Several times in my life I have known there was such a plan, but I did not know how to find and follow it.

Back in February we were making plans to move to the Coast in order to be closer to the specialists that could possibly help Larry with his medical needs. But there would be a benefit for me also because I would be living closer to my sister who had lost her husband two years earlier. In my mind, if something did happen to Larry, Eleanor and I would be company for each other.

Now I was back in Castlegar. Standing at the top of the stairs, a sense of my aloneness comes rushing over me; for a brief moment I almost panic. I think, "I'll go crazy, sitting here all alone." Then I recover and I think, "I can make it, I'll find things to do."

I wrote in my journal, "God does work in mysterious ways His wonders to perform. I still believe God has a plan for my life, and in the working out of His plan He has turned my life upside down completely. Nothing is the same as we planned."

How easily we say, "I want God's will in my life," and we don't really know what His will may be, how hard it may be or what circumstances we will go through in the working out of His will. I prayed, "Lord, You gave me peace when You took Larry home, now I need to have the peace that only You can give in the darkest night and in the midst of the biggest storm I encounter."

Jesus said the peace that He gives would not be as the world gives; that which is subject to circumstances and feelings. The peace He promised is that which is constant in spite of what is happening around us. It is an inner awareness that God is still in control; He will bring us through as He has so many times before. I need to hold on to the confidence that God never takes anything away without a reason. What He gives in its place is better than what He took away.

The unknown generates fear. It doesn't need to be bad; it only has to be unknown. If the Lord is my Shepherd, I can walk through the valley of the shadow of death because He is my security. I ask myself, "Do I really know Jesus so I can follow Him where I have never been before and feel safe just because He's there?"

Once again, I stand at a crossroad. There are many avenues that are open; which one is the best one—the right one? I don't want to make a wrong choice; I have done enough of that in the past. The future is before me; I choose to follow Jesus who knows me, and He knows the way I should take. I need to communicate with Him.

In my prayer time I ask the questions, "For what purpose was I born? "In his book *The Secret Life of the Unborn Child*, Dr. Thomas Verny explores the life of the child in the womb. The unborn child is aware of the surroundings outside the womb before he comes into the world, and he is very aware of the mothers' emotions. From what my mother told me about my birth, I don't think I wanted to be born.

Chapter 3
Raging Waters

"If it had not been the Lord Who was on our side, when men
rose up against us, then the waters would have overwhelmed us
and swept us away, the torrent would have gone over us;"

—Psalm 124:2, 4

I was supposed to be born on September 3, but I arrived on September 10, 1936, in Simpson, Sask. My father was a Norwegian immigrant, and my mother was a Canadian born farm girl. They met at a dance, and my mom was swept off her feet by this blond, blue-eyed foreigner. My dad was a hired man on a farm, but after some months of courting they decided to get married. On November 15, 1935, they were married in Saskatoon, Sask.

With no home and no skills they went to work on a farm as the hired man and the hired girl. My mother was paid $5 a month. The farm was sold just before I was due to be delivered, so Mrs. Fines, the farmer's wife, took my mother to the nearest hospital to await my arrival. I can say I was born in a bank because up until that summer the building had been a bank before it became a hospital.

Six boys had been born there, and I was baby number 7, the first girl. Mom was in labor from Monday evening to Thursday evening at nine o'clock. I was breeched, and finally Dr. Rose used forceps to turn me, and

20

I was born. He told my mom, "Be thankful that you are alive and the baby too." Later, my mom told us that when she was near death, she was walking through a beautiful green meadow. She had never seen such a beautiful green meadow, and the flowers there were of such magnificent colors. She wanted to stay there and rest.

Mom's description of me was that I was blond, blue eyed, and fair skinned, like my dad. Mom had jet-black hair, dark brown eyes, and light olive skin. Ten days later when Dad came to get us from the hospital, he insisted Mom drive the car and he would hold the baby. He had brought baby clothes and a flannelette blanket. He had also brought liquor to celebrate with my grandfather.

Until I was seven months old, we lived with Mom's parents, Nana and Grandpa Phillips, on their farm. When they decided to leave the farm, my grandparents gave their machinery, cattle, and three horses to Mom and Dad who had rented a farm. Water was scarce, and Dad had to haul water for the animals and themselves.

In the three years they were on the farm, they never had a crop. My dad was not a good farmer. He would stay in town drinking with his buddies and come home late at night to milk the cows. My dad wouldn't let Mom milk the cows. They barely existed. While Mom was living on cottage cheese, she was nursing me.

Two weeks after my third birthday, my brother, Orval, was born. A year later we left the farm and moved into the town of Watrous. On May 18, 1941, my dad and his brother, Sig, were walking past an army recruiting office in Saskatoon. WW2 was in full swing, and on a whim my dad went in and joined the Canadian Armed Forces. He was thirty-four years old, but he joined the army in order to have a job.

Early family pictures reveal the sadness of that event as my mother, pregnant with a third child, posed with her soldier husband and two little children. My mom had memories of a May 24 parade with a band playing in the distance. She could hear the sound as she was on her knees scrubbing the floor. A neighbor couple walked by all dressed up. Mom felt she had nothing nice to wear.

What I remember about that time was ration books, train loads of soldiers passing through, and the night my father was one of those soldiers leaving. He went for training to Fort Garry, Manitoba, and while he was stationed there we moved into a small apartment in Portage La Prairie. My mom wanted us all to spend some time together before Dad was sent to England.

We took the train back to Watrous to be near Mom's family before the baby came. It was a good thing we went back then because my sister, Eleanor, not due until October, was born early, one day after my fifth birthday, September 11. I remember the pretty pink socks my grandmother bought me when my sister was born.

When Eleanor was six weeks old, Dad came home one last time before going overseas. It would be five years before we would all be together again. My mom was alone with three small children. Her neighbors, pastors of a new Pentecostal Church in town invited her to come to the church with her children.

Mom heard the gospel, and she accepted Christ as her Savior, a decision she never regretted and one she never turned back on. One thing that was emphasized was prayer for healing. I was scheduled for surgery for my appendix, but Mom believed God could heal me, so I was anointed with oil and prayed for. I remember the doctor coming and Mom telling him I would not need the surgery. The appendix problem came back the next year and I had the surgery.

Unfortunately, the church did not gain much support in the years they were there; the pastor left and that church disbanded. So Mom was ripe for other teachings. My grandmother was a Jehovah's Witness, and soon they were picking Mom and three children up for home studies. They let me read, so I thought this was great.

I even went door to door with pamphlets by myself and ran for my life when a woman crumpled the paper up in my face. They didn't celebrate Christmas or birthdays, and we couldn't watch a parade or salute the flag. I had already felt disappointment when I learned there is no Santa Claus. I vowed to tell my children the truth.

Eventually the war ended in May 1945, and my dad came back to Canada. I'd like to say our dad came home, and we all lived happily ever after, but that would not be true. This stranger we called "dad" arrived in Watrous by train in January 1946. I was ten years old, Orval was seven, and Eleanor was five. We didn't know him, and we soon discovered that he did not want to know us. Mom told us years later that he wanted to put us in an orphanage, and she said no.

Once in a while Dad would pay some attention to my sister, but as far as my brother and I were concerned we were constantly made to feel worthless and unwanted. My brother has memories of when he was about seven years old, sitting on a log near the chicken coup. There was an old Case tractor nearby with steel wheels. As he watched the baby chicks running in the pen he was whittling on a piece of wood, feeling so alone. Once, when Mom was in hospital and we went to stay with Nana, my dad ate my brother's pet rabbit.

We all grew up with a low self-image, ashamed of who we were partly because of being children of the town drunk. I felt that I was not as good as everyone else; somehow I was flawed. This affected me for many years. I never held Dad's hand or sat on his knee, and I don't remember having a conversation with him about anything.

As a father he was negligent, and as a husband he was even worse. He couldn't speak without a long string of curse words whether he was drunk or sober. He called Mom terrible names and accused her of awful things. My Mom always protected us from Dad's anger.

If we needed any discipline, she was the disciplinarian. I do not remember being strapped by Dad, but Mom told me that when I was about three or four years old, my dad had hit me with a leather strap; and at the end of the strapping, he saw my bare legs and hit me one more time across my legs. Mom never let him touch me again.

We also grew up with a poverty complex because we were poor. Dad had a job as a mechanic, and he made good money, but he spent his money at the beer parlor drinking with his buddies. As a fourteen-year-old in Norway, my dad had run away to sea, and he had learned to drink like the sailors. Alcohol had been a problem before he was in the army, but now it was an even bigger problem for us.

When I was in grade four, I had a fainting spell at school. At night I dreaded the moment when the light would be put out because then the room would close in on me, and I would cry out that I was dying. In those days we didn't go to the doctor often, but Mom knew this was serious, so she took me to see him. He said I was extremely anemic. I could not finish the two months left of that school year; I had to rest most of the time and take medication. Over the summer I recovered and was ready for grade five in the fall.

We stopped going to Jehovah's Witnesses and started going to the Lutheran church, the state church of Norway. Dad had been christened as a baby, and I had also been christened in the Lutheran church when I was a baby. Mom thought it might help Dad, but he didn't go very often. We also went to the Salvation Army in the afternoon and evening because Mom liked the faster music.

In the summer when we had our old Ford car, we would go down to Manitou Lake. The water was full of minerals and very buoyant. I could float or dog paddle in it. It tasted terrible, and you thought you were going to die when you got a mouthful. When we had money to pay for it we could go in one of the indoor pools which were nicer and warmer than swimming in the lake, and sometimes we could even have a hotdog there which always smelled so wonderful.

The few times my dad was with us he insisted on driving even when he was drunk. One night he was pulled over for driving on the wrong side of the road. Although we knew there were bottles of liquor in the car, he told the policeman that he had not been drinking. Mom had wanted to drive, but he wouldn't let her.

Our winter fun was skating at the skating rink. One of our neighbors taught me to skate. He went around the rink holding me up until I could skate by myself, and he even taught me how to skate when turning corners. I enjoyed skating, and it was something we did as often as we could. One winter we even had a small patch of ice on the prairie near our house that we skated on.

Christmas was anything but joyful. The saying "Always winter, never Christmas" pretty much describes it. Because of the former JW teaching that Christmas is a pagan holiday, we are forbidden to take part in; Mom felt guilty if we had a tree and an orange in our stocking, but she would do it for us kids. For my dad the liquor was more abundant, so he was wilder, and we learned to hate it.

One Christmas, just before the stores closed, Mom sent my six-year-old sister into the beer parlor to bring Dad out with some money before he spent it all. My sister says she was so scared when she had to walk in there and find Dad. It was so dark, and all the drunks were leering at her. She was the only one my dad would come out for, so she was the one that was sent in to coax him out.

He was not happy about the interruption, so he came out cursing and swearing, but he went to the hardware store with us and waited while Orval, Eleanor, and I each picked out a present. I remember walking up and down the aisles looking at the toys and trying to pick out something nice that wouldn't cost too much. The storekeeper waited patiently while we decided on our gifts, and then Dad paid for them, acting like he was such a benevolent dad.

We never went on holidays like other people talked about, but once in a while we would take the train to Saskatoon and visit our relatives. That was an adventure because of all the sights and sounds of the big city. The train would rumble along over a big long bridge, and finally we would arrive at our destination. Then we would ride on a streetcar to go to Uncle's apartment building.

In the early morning, before it was light out, we would hear the clip-clop of the milkman's horse, and in the afternoon the bread man would take his horse and cart, clip-clopping down the street. After breakfast we would go to the big department stores. We didn't buy much, but there was so much to look at. Part of the fun was taking the elevator or the escalator to different floors. Once we went to a theater to see a movie with Shirley Temple in it. The most exciting trip of all was when we took the train to Saskatoon to see Princess Elizabeth and Prince Philip when they went through.

One blessing that was a reprieve from our sad home life was when we could stay with our grandparents. Nana and Grandpa Phillips were a stabilizing force in our very uncertain existence. Grandpa was twenty years older than Nana and always in pain. When my mom was seven years old her Dad had an accident with a horse which resulted in one leg being amputated. He had a stump with a wooden leg. He would never say good-bye; he'd always say, "So long."

Sometimes he would joke with us a bit, but most of the time he didn't pay attention to us unless we were doing something we shouldn't be doing. Playing on the rickety wooden well or climbing the tree to get on the shed roof was sure to get us in trouble. Nana was the one we really felt love from. They were not rich financially, but as a child I was not aware of any lack there because Nana always made everything seem so special.

Eating sandwiches made with watercress from her garden and homemade bread, and drinking tea from our saucers was like heaven to us. She told us stories of her childhood in England, and sometimes she would sing a little *la la la* or dance a little jig around the kitchen. A special event was when we would sit very quietly in the dimly lit kitchen, waiting for the little mouse to come out and run across the floor which it always did much to our delight. That was a highlight.

Sometimes Nana would talk to us about the kingdom, and we listened, but we didn't understand it. Mom had taught me how to read music and chord so I would play the old, pump organ and sing from the Jehovah's Witness song book *Take Sides with Jehovah*.

The Lutheran church and the Salvation Army were also lifelines for normalcy. My mom found good friends in the Salvation Army officers who were stationed at the Watrous Corps.

We had "new" clothes when boxes of clothes were given to us from them. They had summer Sunday school picnics and lively Christmas concerts in the winter. They always had a Santa at the concert. I didn't believe in Santa, but I enjoyed singing *Jingle Bells* while waiting for him to come and give out the candy bags.

I was afraid of my father, and I was concerned about my mom who was the main caregiver for the family. Somehow we always seemed to have something to eat even if it was bread and milk with pepper and salt or brown sugar on it. I saw her furrowed brow at times, but as a child I did not understand the stress of what she was going through as she worked to provide for our daily needs.

However, God was there with us in spite of seeming evidence to the contrary. In the next few years I would meet Him more than once in ways that I had never heard of. He was about to show me His awesome power which would be something I would remember for the rest of my life.

Chapter 4
God Is Surely There!

"Behold, I am doing a new thing; now it springs forth; do
You not perceive and know it, and will you not give heed to it?"

—Isaiah 43:19 (AMP)

In the words of the catechism, salvation was taught by the Lutherans; but in the Salvation Army Sunday School, it was more personal, especially on Penitent Sunday. That day they would say that anyone who had not asked Jesus to be their Savior should come to the front, kneel at the altar, and pray. I didn't know if I should go forward or not, so I asked my mom.

She was surprised that I questioned it and answered, "Yes, don't you remember kneeling down and doing that when you were five?" It continued to bother me, and I was concerned that I might not go to heaven; so one night, in my bed, I said, "Lord Jesus, I don't remember asking You to be my Savior before, so I want to do it now. Amen."

I was about twelve years old when I had my first encounter with the Living God. Mom still longed for the Pentecostal services, so when she heard about the Living Waters Camp and the wonderful, spirit-filled services happening there, she loaded us children in our old, black Ford car, and we drove down to the camp for the day.

I didn't remember much about the earlier Pentecostal services when I was younger, but I knew this was different from the Lutheran and the

27

Salvation Army that I went to now. The music was livelier, and there was clapping and sometimes shouting out "Amen!" which never happened in Lutheran services. Everyone seemed happy and enthusiastic as they sang the songs. The preaching was different too.

At the end of the service people were asked to come to the front if they wanted prayer for healing. From the time he was ten months old my brother had suffered with seizures so, Mom told him to go in the healing line. Mom insisted that I should go in the line to be prayed for as well. I didn't want to go, but I obediently went.

I was standing next to my brother in the line in front of the altar. There were people standing behind us and the men who were praying for people came down the line and anointed each one with oil before they prayed. When Orval was anointed and prayed for, he just stood there, and then he walked back to his seat. We realized later that he was totally and wonderfully healed.

When they laid hands on me, I felt a force which I cannot explain. I did not stand; I went down, overwhelmed with the strong presence of Almighty God. I could not stand in His presence which surrounded and overpowered me. I went down under the power of God, flat on my back in the shavings at the altar, completely held there by an unseen cloud. I stayed there for a few minutes; I did not get up until the cloud lifted. I knew it was God, and His power was awesome!

I know that God is real; I've met Him, and no one and nothing can convince me otherwise. Orval walked away totally healed; he never had any seizures after being prayed for. I was not healed, but I never forgot what the power of God felt like. Years later I was reminded of this incident when we were living up north and without a church. I knew God was real and that He still cared about me.

My second encounter with the power of God was also at Living Waters Camp. This time I was in the children's service which was held in a smaller building. I don't remember the Bible story or what the lady told us about the Holy Spirit, but I still remember these words: "The Holy Spirit is here; all you have to do is close your eyes, open your mouth, and breathe Him in."

When she came and asked me if I knew Jesus as my Savior, I said, "Yes." Then I closed my eyes, opened my mouth, and breathed in. Immediately tears were running down my cheeks, and I was speaking in a language that was unknown to me. I had not been taught about the baptism of the Holy

Spirit or even about the Holy Spirit Himself, but I knew this was real, and once more I knew it was God.

The adults heard the noise of the children crying and speaking in tongues, and they came over and watched from the outside through the open windows. My mom was one of the adults watching, and she was happy for me. She wanted more of God in her own life and was overjoyed when shortly after that, during the camp meeting, she had the same experience. Mom had a deep love for God and wanted us to follow Him. She did her best to instill respect for His Word.

I did well in school and even dreamed of being a teacher someday. Grade seven was especially memorable. The classroom was a combination of grade sevens and grade eights. Our teacher had been in WW2, so in our music time we sang lots of wartime songs like "I've Got Sixpence" or "It's a Long Way to Tipperary" and "Roll Out the Barrel" as well as other songs.

For the afternoon readings, each grade had their own book, and we took turns each day. I was chosen to be the reader for grade seven. I loved going to the local library, and in the summer when the Library closed for a couple of weeks I always took a load of books home.

That year my mom went to the hospital with pneumonia, and we stayed with Nana and Grandpa. Nana braided my wet hair at night, and in the morning we combed it out. I added to my new look for school by wearing some of my Aunt Eileen's old lipstick and nail polish I found in a cupboard. I thought I looked beautiful.

The next summer we moved to Prince Albert. We sold the house in Watrous and bought a war-time house on First Street. For my grade eight I went to Connaught School which was just down the street from where we lived. I made friends with Geraldine, a girl in the neighborhood who was a few years older than me. Gerry had red hair and a temper to match, and she fascinated me.

One day, in a temper tantrum, she threw her little sister's table and chairs out of an upstairs window. She was not like any other girls I knew. She was dating two different men and trying to decide between them. She loved music, and she would come over and sing while my mom played the piano. She went forward in a tent meeting because she was attracted to one of the men in the quartet, and she wanted him to pray with her. I liked going places with her.

We started attending the Pentecostal Church, and I made friends with some of the girls there. One girl, who was a year younger than me, became my best friend. She lived a few blocks from me, and I was always scared if I came home from her place after dark because I had to pass a big sand pit. Running past that pit, I could always hear footsteps that sounded like someone was behind me.

Sometimes on a Saturday Shirley and I would ride bikes through town and across the bridge over to the TB Sanitarium. I didn't own a bike, so I would knock on a door that had a bike in the yard and ask if I could borrow the bike. They always said, "Yes." On the way back from the Sanitarium, sometimes we would buy a bag of popcorn from the street vendor who always put extra butter on it.

One time when we were riding bikes two boys on bikes harassed us. The boy beside me rode too close, and the chains caught causing our bikes to fall. When I got up and started toward him he started running. I can still see the look of fear on his face. I was fast on my feet, and I was right behind him. He was saved from my wrath when I heard Shirley laughing; I stopped running and started laughing too.

Shirley and I sang duets on *The Sunshine Hour*, a radio program for children, and we sometimes sang a special number for the Young People's Service. My mom took us to another small church that had an affiliation with the Sharon Bible College in North Battleford. My brother and I often sang on their radio program on Sunday evening.

My mom cleaned offices to pay for books and clothes I needed for high school. I took grades nine and ten at the Prince Albert Collegiate. Every morning I had a twenty minute bus ride to the bottom of the hill, and then I walked up the steps and around the court house to the school which was on the next street. Waiting for buses and walking up the hill was very cold in winter.

I was interested in boys, but my mom was very strict. In my grade nine classroom, a boy named Ralph sent me a note, and I answered. Our classmates got a large charge out of our puppy love and wrote on the blackboard, "Romeo and Juliet, Ralph and Janna." I didn't know much about him except that his dad raised chickens and that they had religious meetings in their home. We wrote notes all year.

In grade ten there was a boy named Karl. We didn't have any classes together, but he would wait for me after school so we could walk down the hill and take the bus together. Karl had nice manners, and he always carried my books. We enjoyed our walking, talking, and sitting together on the bus. I knew Mom would not let me go out with him because he was an Air Cadet, and she hated the military.

There was an outdoor skating rink a few blocks from our house. It was a blessing that we all had skates as we enjoyed skating to music at that rink. We also went to hockey games on Saturday night when we could. One night Shirley and I cheered for the Saskatoon team instead of PA just to see what would happen. The people around us were very hostile; they thought we were from Saskatoon.

In the summer our church held a baptismal service at Shell Lake which was some distance away from Prince Albert. Mom had decided we should go and be baptized, so in obedience to her I was among those who were baptized in the lake. Although I understood the significance of baptism and it was meaningful I think it would have meant more if I had made the decision to do it.

That same summer, Helen, Shirley, and I went to Living Waters for youth camp. Shirley's parents drove us there and put up a tent for us. It was my first experience tenting, and I really enjoyed it. We got up early enough for breakfast once and ended up on KP duty, so after that we would buy something in the canteen the night before and get up at the last minute, eat fast, and run for chapel.

The evening services were wonderful times of refreshing for me. There was such a hunger within me for more of God. Every evening I could hardly wait for the altar call, a time of praise and worship that would take place around the altar after the main service was over. At the end of the service, Helen and Shirley would leave to go and hang out with the boys, and I would head for the altar. I wanted to spend time in God's presence. I couldn't get enough of Him.

One evening I was so caught up in worship that I was oblivious to time. I was praising the Lord, kneeling there in His presence for some time. I felt like I'd been lifted to heaven. When I was telling the other young people from our church about it, one of the boys said to me, "You will set the church on fire if you go back like that." The last night of camp at the fireside I dedicated my life to serve the Lord. That was a mountain top experience for me.

When camp was over, Mom, Orval, and Eleanor came and picked me up, and we went to visit Nana and Grandpa in Watrous. My glow soon wore off with the tension between my grandma and my mom who couldn't set aside their religious differences. Like the disciples coming down from the mountaintop experience with Jesus, there was the valley and the demons to deal with.

When we got back to Prince Albert, the fire in me was out. Life was the same as it was before camp. However, my dad's drunkenness was worse than ever. Many times when he was violent, throwing things and making threats, Mom would get us out of bed in the middle of the night; and we would stand outside in the backyard until Dad finally went to sleep and it was safe to go back to bed.

Then one day everything changed, my dad's brother, Sigurd, came for a visit. I didn't remember him, although I had seen him when I was a young child. He told us he was no longer an alcoholic, he had become a Christian, and he was living a very different life now. He wanted to help my dad turn his life around too, so he invited us to move to Prince Rupert where he and his family now lived.

It sounded good to them; so Mom and Dad sold the house, the furniture, and other things. We packed up clothes and a few special treasures, and with high expectations we got on the train headed for Prince Rupert, the land of hope. Like the pilgrims of old, we looked forward to the wonderful life ahead.

As we had a stopover in Edmonton, this gave us another new experience, that of staying in a hotel. We did some shopping for new clothes, and the next day being Sunday, Mom found a church for us to go to. I remember that she fell asleep a couple of times, and I was a little embarrassed. I understand it now—the stress of everything and the weariness of the trip this far. The next day we boarded the train for the last part of our journey, finally arriving at our destination on September 3, 1953.

As we arrived in Prince Rupert, we were greeted with rain. I soon learned that rain was normal weather; umbrellas were taken with us even if the sun was shining when we started out. We had moved from sunny Saskatchewan, where rain happened once in a while in the summer, to rainy Rupert where it could rain in the summer or winter and the sun appeared once in a while.

At fifteen years of age I could not have envisioned the course my life was now on. To me, it was an adventure, and I looked forward to the future with great anticipation. I was sure that everything from now on would be wonderful. My mom was very hopeful and seemed to share my enthusiasm.

Chapter 5
Rivers Of Disappointment

"By the rivers of Babylon, there we (captives) sat down,
yes, we wept—on the willow trees in the midst of Babylon
we hung our harps.—How shall we sing the Lord's song
in a strange land?"

—Psalm 137:1-4 (AMP)

My uncle met us at the train and took us home to meet the family whom we had not seen for ten years. The two oldest girls, Jonna and Edith, were close to my age; and the other two girls, Marie and Ann, were close in age to Orval and Eleanor. We didn't have many classes together at school, but we spent time after school being together, and we went to each other's youth groups.

When my dad got a job as a mechanic in Rupert Motors we moved into a rented house. I was able to get a job working in the hospital after school and weekends where Jonna was working. The Pentecostal church was our home church, but I went with my cousins to their church sometimes.

One girl I became friends with in our church was Madeline. Our mothers were friends, and sometimes we would be invited to their house for coffee after church. One evening Madeline's cousin, Dallas, was there, and I was introduced to him. He was six years older than me, and he

33

worked in the pulp mill at Port Edward. That night he gave me a ride home in his car.

Although there was a mutual attraction we were always part of a group. When we started dating it was double dating with Jonna and Dallas's cousin, Roy. We talked about getting married someday, but we had a romantic idea about being married. We did not know what we were getting into. We never discussed money, children, etc. Just before graduation we became engaged. We planned the wedding, not the marriage.

I told myself I loved him and I wanted to marry him, but when I brought my beautiful satin wedding dress home and hung it up I felt scared. I thought about backing out, but the invitations had gone out, and I felt I couldn't change anything now.

My parents signed their consent and on September 6, 1955, we were married. After the reception, we went to our suite and discovered we were locked out and had to crawl in a window. Someone had played tricks, spilling ground coffee in the bed, hiding kitchen items, and putting the bed up on cans.

One Sunday morning shortly after we were married, Dallas decided he wasn't going to church. When we were dating he never complained about it, but now he said he didn't like the preacher or the church. He shocked me further by saying what he didn't like about my family. Where did this come from?

Although I had met his parents, I didn't really know much about his family background. Later I learned of his European background from the grandfather and previous generations where it is customary for the father to rule the family. His mother, from a Quaker background, was a very submissive and gentle lady who allowed the father to make all the decisions.

I was so young, and I didn't have any idea what marriage should look like. I knew my parent's kind of marriage wasn't what I wanted, but I didn't have any example to follow. I never read any books on marriage, and the romance books I read, boy met girl, they got married, and they lived happily ever after. He had never said the words *I love you*, but I was so naive that I saw the mutual attraction as being love. Oh, what a fool I was.

Now I felt betrayed, trapped in a terrible nightmare. "Why did he marry me if he felt like that?" I wished that I had never married him, but it was too late to turn back. We could have come to some understanding by talking about everything, but when I tried to say anything he said he wouldn't "argue." What I might think or say was not important; the case was closed. How sad and prideful to believe your way of thinking is the only way.

So now my life would go on but without an anticipation of a wonderful life together. Instead, we settled into a routine of existence, living together but no camaraderie. When we were with family or friends everything seemed normal on the surface, but the enjoyment of each other's companionship was missing.

Church had always been an important part of my life, and now it became even more so. That was the place where I was validated, made to feel like I was worth something, that my life counted after all. From that time on I went alone. I was young, and my future was ahead of me. What I dreamed of someday having wasn't there, but I was determined to live my life.

When I found out I was pregnant, we were happy about that. Years later I found out what a miracle this was as adhesions from the appendix surgery when I was six years old had grown through my tubes, making it difficult for me to get pregnant. This baby was wanted and already loved by both of us.

I worked at Kelly Douglas until a month before the baby came. The night before his birth, I walked the floor with my little terrier, Friday, beside me. Eleanor was staying with me while Dallas was working nights. At 6:30 AM I called the doctor who told me to go to the hospital. Then I phoned Dallas, and he told me a cab would get there faster than he could drive the ten miles home, but he made it there before the cab.

On June 26, 1956, we welcomed our baby boy; and we named him Dwayne. He had fair hair and blue eyes like my dad. I thought he was the most beautiful baby ever born. Dallas told my mom that he was glad the baby would change in looks. Dwayne was a good-natured baby who loved to laugh. He was adored by all the grandparents and by his Aunt Eleanor who came to help when we came home from the hospital. He was my mom's first grandchild, so he was very special to her.

It was a long walk; but almost every Sunday, rain or shine, I would put Dwayne in the carriage and walk to church. When the new pastors of the Evangelical Free Church moved into the house across the street from us, they invited us to go to church with them, which we did. I also helped in the youth group.

At one year old Dwayne was walking, and soon after that he was running and getting into mischief. He enjoyed having stories read to him, and at two years old he would tell me the stories as we read. He had a vivid imagination and would add details like the three bears' porridge was Sunny Boy.

He was a daddy's boy and would ask all day if Daddy was coming home soon. Sometimes his dad would play hide and seek in the house with him, and that was the highlight of his day. He would "hide" just out of sight, and his excitement and laughter when he was "found" always had us laughing too. When he started talking we thought everything he said was so clever. I began keeping a journal of all his cute sayings.

In the spring of 1959 we packed up our furniture and belongings and moved to Berwyn, Alberta. We stayed with Nona and Harry Aspin until we bought a small house on a lot in Berwyn. It had been a garage which had been insulated and made into two rooms. There was a small kitchen and one larger room which was our living room with a curtained off bedroom.

Dwayne's crib was at the end of our bed, but he liked to sleep in our bed, so he would tell us animals were looking in. One time he said, "A mouse is looking in the window to see if anyone is home. Can I come in your bed?" At three years old he had a very vivid imagination which we took pride in.

Dallas wasn't working, so he looked after Dwayne, and I got a job in the CIBC bank. Shirley Aspin who worked there gave me a reference. We became good friends, and we both learned to drive by taking her dad's old Dodge car on the farm roads to practice our driving skills. Shirley and I had a lot of laughs together.

The next summer we sold the Berwyn property and traded our furniture for a 28-foot long holiday trailer which we parked in a trailer court in Grimshaw. Dallas finally got a job at Swan Hills with the Grimshaw Trucking Company. He stayed there during the week with friends and came home on the weekend.

When Dallas heard that a pulp mill was hiring in Castlegar, he applied for a job and was hired. We were happy to have the job but very sad about leaving our friends. Our time there was so short, and yet we had so many unforgettable moments with Basil and Dollye, Harry and Nona, Dallas's brother, George, and his soon-to-be wife, Joyce. I would also miss Shirley, my pal for getting into mischief!

In September 1960 we hitched the trailer to our pickup truck and set out for Castlegar. We took the Kootenay Lake ferry and traveled the winding road without any trouble, but when we got to Trail, we had a problem with the Cominco hill. Our truck stalled, and I had to run to a garage at the bottom of the hill and get someone to pull us to the top.

Finally, we arrived safely in Castlegar, parked the trailer in a trailer park, and that was our home for that winter. We found a church home and became friends with the pastors, Roy and Lois Webb. Lois was like a big sister, teaching me how to bake bread and sew my own clothes. I became involved in teaching Sunday school, and I was the youth leader for five years.

Mike and Florence Wolfe, who were the age of our parents, were like family, and we often spent Christmas and other holidays together. Florence was also Dwayne's Sunday school teacher, and she enjoyed his responses to her story telling. When she told the story of how God made clothes for Adam and Eve from animal skins, Dwayne said He should have used kangaroos so they could have pockets. He wasn't joking.

The vow I made as a child to tell my children the truth about Santa Claus nearly got me in trouble as Dwayne told the kids in his kindergarten class that Santa Claus died. I had told him the story of St. Nicholas, alias Santa Claus, who gave gifts to the poor, and that after he died, the parents carried on the legacy. The teacher phoned me on that one!

We didn't socialize much, but we were friends with Lorraine and Harold from the Prince Rupert church. One time the four of us went to Harrop and rented horses to go on a trail ride there. The men knew all about horses, and Lorraine may have ridden before, but I had never been on a horse in my life, and I was nervous. In the beginning the horses followed the trail, but suddenly, my horse left the trail, went down on to a field going under all the low branches on the trees. Harold rode down to my rescue, stopped the horse, and got me off.

To other people our marriage may have looked all right. We never fought about anything because our conversation was always on general topics. Dallas made the money, so he handled the paychecks. On payday we bought groceries together and he paid bills, but he seldom gave me money to buy something for myself or for Dwayne. I sold Avon, babysat, and cleaned house for other people to make money.

One winter as I was driving past the mall parking lot, my next-door neighbor was driving out on to the road. She could not stop and ended up side swiping me. Her insurance was going to pay for it, but when I got home and told Dallas about the accident I had to give him the keys to the car. I wasn't allowed to drive the car for months after that.

I loved the Lord, and I loved my son, but I didn't know how to have a proper relationship with my husband. It was a parent-child relationship; he made the rules, and I followed them. We couldn't communicate because I was never allowed to say how I felt about anything; he called it arguing. I didn't hate him, but I didn't know how to break the barrier to communication.

We did some communicating when I found out that Dallas was spending time with another woman. There were warning bells before this, but I didn't want to believe it. When I faced him with the facts, he tried to deny that there was anything going on, but I didn't believe it. At first I was very angry. Then I was extremely depressed; I really wondered why I was living. I thought of taking Dwayne and leaving Dallas, but a book I read stopped me.

Chapter 6
The Valley Of Weeping

"Passing through the valley of weeping
they make it a place of springs;"

—Psalm 84:6 (AMP)

God works in mysterious ways his wonders to perform. I read a book by Frances Parkinson Keyes, one of my favorite authors. The story was about a lady who was in circumstances similar to mine. She had taken her child and left her husband, but everything did not work out very well for her or for her child. Reading that book made me realize how harmful it might be for Dwayne if I took him away from his dad, so I decided to stay. Our lives went on as they had before, and in time the woman and her husband moved away, and we put it behind us.

Our little boy was growing up, he was going to school, and he already knew his letters and numbers because we played Flinch and other table games with him. He liked things to be neat and orderly and took pride in his appearance. He even had ideas that I should wear my hair long and straight, which I never did. He was very caring and liked to help others. He befriended a mentally challenged boy, helping him at Cubs and patiently teaching him how to dial a phone and other things.

We had always wanted more children but never seriously considered adopting. In taking care of someone's baby girl for three months, we became

39

so attached to her and she to us, we realized we could love any baby, so we decided to adopt a baby girl to complete our family. When Dwayne was eight years old, we made an application to adopt.

About nine months later, on April 19 the social worker brought us pictures of a seven-month-old baby girl. The scripture in my devotional that morning was "Having predestinated us unto adoption of children." Although that verse is not speaking about adoption like we were doing, I felt it was confirmation from the Lord that this was the baby for us.

A few days later we picked up our baby whom we named Brenda. The story of how we got Baby Brenda was written in her baby book and became her favorite story which we read to her often. She never made strange or cried; she was our baby right from the beginning. A check up with our doctor revealed she was very anemic. We had been told she had a feeding problem, but she had no problem with any of the baby food, formula, or the prescribed liquid iron she was given.

Brenda was a bright little girl with an interest in bugs, worms, and small wild animals. When her dad caught a pocket gopher she wanted to take it to her friend's house to show them. She named our black cat Ben after the bear Gentle Ben, and she and Ben got along very well, even sharing puffed wheat on the floor together.

She had a good imagination and liked to pretend she was Mrs. Jones who came to visit. Some of the questions she asked made me think she would be a nurse someday. We looked at pictures in the Books of Knowledge and counted them to answer "How many ribs do we have?" then we looked at other pictures of body parts, learning their names.

Our house was now too small. Originally, a summer house with one bedroom and a sunroom, which was Dwayne's bedroom, it was no longer adequate for our growing family. We were going to add on to it, but Mike Wolfe advised us to tear it down and build a Prefabricated home, so we did; we built a very nice three-bedroom Beaver home.

We were the ideal family—camping with the kids in the summer and once or twice a year visiting family at the Coast or Alberta. One winter, Dallas bought himself a ski-doo, and on weekends he would go out with some of his friends from the mill. Occasionally the kids and I would go with him ski-dooing at his friend's place. We also took the kids to hockey games, something we enjoyed as a family.

Christmas time was always difficult as most of the time I didn't have much money for gifts. Thank God for the family allowance! Dallas didn't like Christmas much, and sometimes he didn't even get out of bed on Christmas day to see the kids open their gifts. Gifts for me were rare. When the mill was on strike Christmas was a real downer.

We decided to sell our house and move to a more central location. We bought a house in Woodland Park close to the school Brenda would go to for her grade two. Out of the blue I got a call from a supervisor at the CIBC. They still had my application from years before and wanted to know if I was interested in working for them. I asked a friend if Brenda could go to their place after school; the money could help them, and as a family we talked about it and decided it would be a good idea.

Two ladies that I knew personally who were close to my age had gone back to college, finished their education, and were now teachers which made me think I was not too old to try it. I decided to enroll at Selkirk College for night school beginning with one course for credit. I chose Psychology because it interested me. The first night I was very nervous, and when the teacher gave us our assignment I wondered what I was doing there, but as time went on I really enjoyed it.

The vast differences in what Dallas and I wanted out of life were becoming more apparent as time went on. He was going to Spokane more frequently for weekends by himself or with his friend from work. He made other excuses for going, but I knew they were going to a certain theater that he had taken me to once.

He heard that his mom was going to Hawaii to a cousin's wedding, so he decided to go with her even though he was not invited. Once again we never discussed it. I was really tired of living together but not sharing life. Dwayne finished high school and had his first job, and I felt he was taken care of, so I made arrangements for a transfer to a CIBC branch at the Coast. Interestingly, Dallas came home early, and he wanted us to stay together, so he agreed we'd go for counseling.

However, he did not like the counselor's questions, and after two sessions of counseling he refused to go again. We came to the conclusion that a new place might help us make a fresh start, so we decided to move to Surrey, BC. There was no transfer immediately available with CIBC, so I applied for a job with the Fraser Valley Credit Union and was hired. Dallas began working as a carpenter's helper.

The following October, when Brenda was eleven years old, I took her to Norway. My brother and sister decided to go with us, and the four of us went to night classes to learn Norwegian before the trip. We flew to Oslo, visited our cousin and her family there, and then flew down to spend two weeks in Kopervik where most of the family lived. Brenda and I stayed with Aunt Gunhild who did not speak much English.

We did not have time to visit each one in their homes, so they rented a hall and everyone came together for an evening of playing games, visiting, and getting to know our Norwegian family. There were fourteen children in my dad's family and only two lived in Canada, so we had many aunts, uncles, and cousins that we had not met before.

My cousin, Nancy, had lived in Canada for a short time, and she spoke English very well. When Brenda and I stayed with her it was interesting to hear the children learning each other's language as they played together. We visited cousin Marit and her family in Stavanger before flying from there to Scotland and then home to Canada. It was a wonderful trip, and I'll always be glad we were able to do that.

One happy occasion for us was Dwayne and Maureen's wedding on September 2, 1978, in Castlegar. Maureen was a beautiful bride, and Dwayne was a handsome groom. Their love for each other was apparent, and I prayed for their happiness. Maureen's parents had moved to Castlegar as we had in 1960 when the mill opened up.

Dallas and I did not have many friends in Surrey, but we did get to know Larry and Ida Spratt, friends of Dallas's brother George and his wife. Spratts had lived in Grimshaw the same year we lived in Berwyn. The men had hunted together, and I had met Ida and their two little girls once, but Larry and I did not remember ever meeting before.

We moved to a house in Delta which was on the bus route and close to Brenda's school. Dallas got a job with Panco Poultry working steady afternoon shifts, Monday to Friday. I worked Tuesday through Saturday, so we only had one day off together. Brenda and I went to church on Sunday morning, which meant we could do something on Sunday afternoon. He liked to barbeque and sometimes did steaks for lunch that day, and then if he felt like it, we might visit someone.

On September 10, 1976, I turned forty, and I felt very depressed. I couldn't see a future with any hope in it. Looking back over my life, there had been so little happiness. The first nineteen years, my childhood and teen years were about survival, and the last twenty-one years of marriage was mere existence. My life had no meaning.

Dallas and I had no real interests in common, and we never had any meaningful conversation. Staying like we were would mean that the years ahead would stretch out in meaningless numbers until in the end I would die, not ever having really lived. I wondered if there was any more to life than this. Other people seemed to have more, and when I was around them I could enjoy a social event, but when I was alone I felt sad and empty.

Although I did not try to change anything, an unexpected turn of events radically turned my life around. I would never be the same again. In October 1978, Dallas surprised me by suggesting that we go our separate ways; he added, "No counseling." In the short time we were together on weekends, he had not suggested this before, but I couldn't see any reason to try to change his mind, so we listed the house with the real estate the next day.

When it finally sold in April 1979, we calmly divided the spoils of our marriage and walked away from our twenty-four years of captivity. We didn't argue about anything; we both wanted out of our miserable existence. If he felt anything, he never talked about it.

What could have been a very negative happening became instead the very catalyst that caused positives in my life. At first I felt tired, stressed from packing, getting an apartment, and moving. There was also the emotional upheaval, the finality of the breakup, the loss of something which could never be recovered.

In my times alone I wept for what was, and I wept for what we could have had. I wept for the uncertainty of the road ahead. At forty-two years of age, what would freedom mean for me? Those who loved me were supportive. My sister and her family were always there for Brenda and me. We spent a lot of time with them.

But something very important in my own growth had begun in the house before we split up. I would get up early in the morning so I could spend time in Bible reading and prayer before going to work. I read through the Bible for the first time in my life. The church I attended stressed the importance of studying the Bible, so I would take notes on the sermons, and on my day off, I would go to my sister's house, and she and I and Vern would study those scriptures.

Wednesday night at the church there was something happening for every age group. Brenda was in the youth choir, and I was in one of the Bible courses. I became secure in my faith, believing that God was holding on to me, not me holding on to Him. I believed that God loved me as I was, and it was not based on my performance.

My story was similar to the parable in Mark 13. For the first forty years I heard the Word; the good seed was sown in my heart, but it never had a strong root. It had been laying dormant all these years.

One Sunday, Pastor Carmont spoke on how we climb with difficulty up the mountain, and when we come down there are those to whom we minister. In the Sunday school that morning, a pastor had spoken from Luke 4 (Isaiah 61): "The Spirit of the Lord God is upon me." The messages reiterated something that I believed the Lord was already impressing on me, that I might be a help to others.

An evangelist who came to our church later spoke on how the Lord has given some people a vision, but He has not brought it to pass yet. His prayer for me was "Help her to see the open door and to walk through it in faith." I didn't know what the future held for me, but I really felt the call of God on my life.

There was no clear indication of what God wanted me to do at this time, so I volunteered wherever I saw a need I could fill. I played the piano at a mission on Carroll Street in Vancouver, and I played the organ at the Salvation Army Harbor Light. I played the piano for a little church in Aldergrove and for a seniors' home in Surrey.

My mind opened up; I was no longer stifled, and I began taking college courses at night to finish my education. The Adolescent Psychology course was good for my own personal development and self-esteem as I learned to accept myself. I attended a Writers Conference in Seattle, WA, which reawakened my interest in writing. I took a course called Ladies Know Your Car, and at the end of the course I could do a tune up on my 1969 Ford.

There were some positive happenings in our family too which brought us joy. One was the birth of my first granddaughter, Ayron, on October 14, 1980. She was blond and beautiful, a replica of her dad as a baby. Then on October 9, 1982, the birth of Dwayne and Maureen's only son, Shawn, completed their family. They were two beautiful children, so different in personality. Ayron was full of energy, always moving and Shawn, so laid back and easy going.

Dallas and I had been married but emotionally separated for twenty-four years; now we were legally separated for almost five years, and he seemed content to go on like this forever. We met for lunch once a month so he could give me the support payment for Brenda, and we would all get together when Dwayne and Maureen came to visit, but he never talked about the past or suggested that we had any future.

Once again I saw my life as endless repetition of old patterns of behavior. I knew we would just keep going around and around like this forever, so when I saw an ad in the paper for a divorce service that was not too expensive I climbed the stairs to their tiny office and started the procedure. I felt ill at one point, could not remember a date and wrote the wrong one, but I wanted to be done.

I did not mean to hurt anyone, but I didn't want to live like this any longer. I had to cut the ties and get on with my life. I was in limbo; I couldn't go back to the oppression of a loveless, empty life, and I was not able to move forward because of the strings of the past. I thought, "If I die tomorrow, the last four and one half years were more worthwhile than all the years before." My abusive childhood plus oppressive married life added up to too many years of wasted life.

Chapter 7
Great Waters

"Your way (in delivering Your people) was through the sea and
Your paths through the great waters;"

—Psalm 77:19 (AMP)

At this time my daughter and I began having challenges. We fought about some of the rules she didn't like. I did not handle that too well. I was brought up with rules which I didn't like either, but I never openly challenged them. My pattern for parenting was what I was brought up with. I know now that we should have talked more. I should have been more open to hearing her point of view. We needed communication.

The stress of the divorce and the challenges with my daughter finally caught up with me, and on December 2, 1983, I went to my doctor with chest pains. The first question he asked me was "Are you under stress?" He was easy to talk to, so I talked about the divorce and my concern about hurting my husband.

I do not know if he was even a believer, but he said something very profound: "God will take care of him." When I told him about my relationship with my daughter, he said, "She will soon move out as she is nineteen now, and your relationship will be better then." I left his office choking back the tears. I felt like I had heard from God.

46

On December 10 an old friend came into the branch where I was working. He was driving into Surrey when he thought of me and decided to ask me out for lunch. I had not seen Larry Spratt much since he had moved out to Clearbrook. The year before this, he had stopped in to tell me that Ida had Alzheimer's, and now he told me she was in a nursing home in Abbotsford.

During lunch he asked me if I would go with him that evening to his company Christmas party. I said yes, so he picked me up later, and we drove out to the party. I didn't know anyone there except his brother, Herb, and his wife, Doreen, who were friendly and seemed all right with me being there with Larry.

When he drove me home that night, I invited him up to my apartment, and over coffee we filled in the past five years. We were two people who had gone through storms which left us scarred and shaken, but we were still standing, determined to make it.

Larry needed to talk. He said he often walked in the park at night crying out to God, feeling lonely and depressed. He talked about their struggles with Ida's sickness undiagnosed for years. They had lost their friends, and people at their church didn't seem to care.

When he left around midnight, he asked if I would like to go out for dinner sometime. I said yes, thinking it would not happen very soon. I wrote in my journal, "I don't know if I could fall in love with him or not. I know that we can talk, and that is something I've always thought would be an excellent ingredient in a relationship."

A few days later I came home from work and was warming up my dinner when I heard the door buzzer. I was surprised to hear Larry's voice. I let him in and invited him to stay for dinner. Larry liked the meal, and a few nights later he showed up at dinnertime again. When you give the saucer of cream to that stray cat, it comes back!

On Saturday evening we went to a Chinese restaurant, and as we were walking in to the restaurant, a five-dollar bill drifted out. I picked it up, and Larry teasingly told everyone later that I grabbed that money and refused to use it to pay for my meal. The girls at work had warned me to make sure I paid for my own meal.

When we were together it felt so right, and when we were apart we looked forward to the next time we could be together. So friendship became love as we built a relationship. In order to spend more time together, I would often drive out to his house for the weekend. His parents were living with him since Ida had gone into the nursing home, so they were our chaperones.

In September 1984, just before my birthday, my dad passed away very suddenly. My sister called me, and we went in to make the arrangements. The last years of his life he lived in a seniors' place in New Westminster. He got drunk and was kicked out of the first place he went into, but my sister was able to get him into another one. She tried to help him as best as she could. Almost every Monday, on my day off, we took him for lunch at Woodwards which he seemed to enjoy.

At the end of his life he quit drinking and smoking, and he was going to church with a couple from a Lutheran church that picked him up every Sunday. He said he found his strength in reading his Bible every day. He never apologized for the kind of father he had been, but he gave us a card on our birthday, signed, "Love, Dad." When we cleaned out his room after his death we found signed cards for us ready for this year. We had a funeral for him and buried him on my birthday. He was seventy-seven years old.

As the months went by, Larry and I were spending more evenings and weekends together, and it was becoming more costly and difficult driving back and forth. Larry was struggling to pay the extra cost for Ida's care besides his other payments. Although asking for help was very stressful, he borrowed money a few times from family members, but when he was told he would have to pay it back that caused more stress because he didn't know how he would do that.

Eventually we came up with the perfect solution. I should move out to Abbotsford to live with Larry. We reasoned it all out; the money I was paying for my apartment could help him pay for Ida's care and other expenses. I would apply for a transfer out to the Abbotsford branch of the Credit Union and drive to my job in Surrey until a transfer came through. Brenda could stay in the Surrey apartment and keep my 1969 Ford for her own use.

I searched the scriptures to see if God had said anything about it. In the Old Testament, I read that men had more than one wife, and I could not find any scripture where God told them it was the wrong thing to do. So I reasoned I could be Larry's second wife. Eventually we would marry, but for now we would live together under common law as husband and wife. I changed my surname to Spratt.

So according to plan, Larry brought a truck to my apartment and moved all my furniture and belongings into his house in Abbotsford. Although I still considered myself a Christian I had embraced what Bonheoffer called "cheap grace" which is salvation without discipleship. I believed I was eternally secure so I could live like I wanted with no consequences. Oh, I had so very much to learn!

Some people in the family voiced their objections to Larry, but he was adamant. We would not listen to anyone else; we were doing what was right for us, and eventually others would have to accept it. Surprisingly, no one said anything to me about our decision.

We honestly wanted to start our life together as right as we could make it, and from the beginning we had good communication. We talked about everything—our past where we had been and how our choices had shaped us and our future goals. We discussed possible ways we could achieve those goals. We were planning a future together—side by side, sharing life.

When Larry was not on the road, we would begin the day with a cup of coffee, reading the Bible, and praying together. Our desire was to build a relationship having God at the center of all we did and from there strengthen the bond we had with each other. We liked being together, and that was our greatest enjoyment whether we were driving somewhere or just sitting by the fireplace at home.

At first everything seemed to be working out as we had hoped it would. We got a better mortgage at the Credit Union, and between us we were able to pay all the expenses. Then the old truck that Larry was driving started breaking down, and the repairs for that were very expensive. The trips didn't always bring in enough money to cover everything we had to pay out even with both of us working.

Trucking was not easy, especially in winter when he would be trying to tarp a load with half frozen tarps. In December 1984, Larry had emergency surgery for a stomach problem. Interestingly, the Lord had provided for our needs ahead of time. For the first time in his life Larry was working for a company that had wage loss benefits, and from December 1984 to May 1985 he collected a good wage.

After Larry's surgery he couldn't do heavy work as he had previously done, so we bought a Nissan pickup truck for him to do light deliveries. I was now working in Abbotsford, so I didn't have to drive as far. We repaid the people he had borrowed from, and we were able to meet our financial obligations, but there was not much left over. In my journal I wrote, "I don't begrudge paying for Ida's care, but I long for something new for myself or Larry instead of only being able to buy necessities, nothing extra."

In Dec 1986, my car blew a head gasket, and we wondered how we would pay for that, but then Larry received a call from the Public Trustee concerning Ida's dad's estate. After a long court battle it was settled, and Ida would receive a small inheritance which would help pay for her care. We had tried not to be concerned; we always prayed about everything, and the Lord never let us down.

Larry and I loved each other, and we were building a relationship. We handled any problems we encountered together, and we grew as we went through them. Although we had not waited for God and had taken matters in our own hands to be together, we believed we were right for each other, and eventually all things would work out. I was free to grow as a person, and that was important to me. For the first time in my life I was writing poetry and journaling often.

In 1987 we sold the house and bought a condo in Abbotsford. It was small but adequate, and we no longer had to worry about the yard work. Larry was having some angina, and he was in the care of a specialist. I applied for a transfer to the accounting department of the Credit Union's head office, which was in Abbotsford.

The morning of February 14, 1988, Larry received a call that Ida had passed away. In the last months she was so deteriorated that Larry would be upset after visiting her. The family and Larry made the arrangements for the memorial. I did not attend as I felt it was important for Larry and his children to grieve together as a family.

We set May 21, 1988, as the date for our wedding and arranged for my former pastor, Rev. Daniel Breen, to marry us in Peoples Church, Surrey, BC. One person in the family objected because he felt we were marrying too soon after Ida's death. We had lived together for four years, and we felt that was long enough to wait.

Two weeks before the wedding, Larry went to see if he could reason with him, but he refused to understand. Larry lost his temper and said things he later regretted and apologized for in a letter. When Larry came home and told me about what transpired in their meeting, I was so angry I sent him a letter which was not so nice. He had never lifted a finger to help Larry in the years when he needed help, but now he could sit in judgment on us with his self-righteous attitude. I lost my cool, and I wasn't sorry!

On Sunday we got together, but nothing was resolved. The next day this was on Larry's mind so much that he had an accident with his truck. At the scene of the accident he was having chest pains, but he refused to go in the ambulance; he came home instead. When he told me what happened, I talked him into going to the emergency to get checked out. However, his truck was damaged and would have to wait for parts from Japan, so we were not sure how he could work.

What seemed to be a bad circumstance actually worked out for our good. The company Larry was working for had been asking him to get a bigger truck because the work was there for it, and we had been praying about it since January without a clear answer. Now, we felt the time was right to get a bigger truck.

The sun shone on May 21, a beautiful day for our wedding. My sister, Eleanor, and Larry's brother, Herb, were our attendants; and my son, Dwayne, walked me down the aisle and gave me away. Our granddaughters, Christy and Ayron, lit the candles. My daughter, Brenda, catered a wonderful wedding lunch. Our parents, siblings, children, family, and friends celebrated with us. Our wedding night was in the Rainbow Country Inn in Chilliwack, and the next day we began our honeymoon trip down to Leavenworth, WA.

We began praying about Larry getting his own operating authority. Don Murray who worked in the government office had always been very helpful whenever Larry needed advice or papers filed, so we asked him if he would help us get all the papers in order. He told us to come to his home the next week, and he would be happy to help us. By Sept 1990 we had our own operating authority under RL & J Ventures, (later incorporated.)

Soon we had more work than we could handle, so we asked Earle Sinkie to come and work for us. Before long there was more work than they could handle, so we hired more drivers. We were growing faster than we could keep up. Larry had a good reputation with the companies, and the dispatchers worked well with him. Larry did all the dispatching for our company, and I did the bookkeeping.

After we were married, Larry and I decided to make a fresh start in a new church, the Evangelical Free Church. We felt very welcome there, made new friends, and enjoyed the social events. We were part of a care group with three other couples which met weekly for Bible study. We also had a monthly Sunday service for a seniors' lodge, playing our instruments and singing hymns with them.

An article in the paper about an AM Toastmasters group piqued my interest, and I decided to join them. The group met in a room in a local restaurant at 7:30 AM. Muffins and coffee were served, and the meeting was finished in time for everyone to go to their various jobs. It was a very interesting experience for me. Speeches were critiqued, all the "ums" were counted, and some videotaping was done so we could see our own presentation which was helpful.

In March 1991, the smoke in the office was getting worse. Then one night I was up for hours just trying to breathe. When I went to my doctor the next day he put me on a medical leave stating on the insurance form that the problem was smoke in the office. The positive outcome from that was a ruling by the board that as of January 1992 there would be no smoking in any of the branches.

In August and September I had diverticulitis, was given antibiotics, and then had a relapse. I felt I could not go through it again, so I asked for prayer from the elders of the church. As the people formed a circle around me, the pastor and the elders anointed me with oil and prayed. I was completely healed; I never had it again.

On a sunny day in July 1991, Brenda and Adrian were married. It was Brenda's wish that her father and I walk her down the aisle, and we were happy to do that for our little girl. Brenda was a beautiful bride, and Adrian was a handsome groom, and the ceremony was very nice. Larry and I and Adrian's parents were asked to read certain portions of scripture during the ceremony which was a very nice way to involve the parents. Afterward they took up residence in Surrey.

Chapter 8
The Fire

"When you walk through the fire, you shall not be burned or scorched, nor shall the flame kindle upon you."

—Isaiah 43:2 (AMP)

One December we decided to go to a Christmas Scandinavian dinner, a fund raiser for the Lutheran summer camp. The Lutefisk and Swedish meatballs were delicious, and the elderly gentleman with his Norwegian accent kept us laughing with Ole and Lena jokes. The evening ended with the beautifully decorated tree being pulled into the center of the room and people walking around the tree, holding hands as they sang carols in English or Norwegian. We enjoyed this so much that we made this an annual event, and every year we took family members or friends with us.

For some unknown reason, I began having bouts of vertigo. The first time it happened I became so weak that Larry called the ambulance. I had lost so much potassium that they gave it to me intravenously in the emergency room which was extremely painful. One time when I was at work I felt it coming on, so I went home before it completely engulfed me. I had four attacks of it that year. Fortunately it never happened when I was driving or in a public place.

When I retired from the Credit Union on May 31, 1992, I left with mixed emotions. I had worked in three branches for a total of eighteen years, and it was like a second home. I liked the people I worked with, and I enjoyed the work in the accounting department. However, our trucking company was growing, and I couldn't do both jobs; I needed to devote more time to our company, so I made that difficult decision.

In time, Larry and I began talking about selling our business and retiring to a quiet place, away from the city. After looking at properties in Alberta, we stopped in Castlegar to visit our children, and Maureen got a listing of properties in this area for us to look at. We found our quiet place—two acres beside a creek in the Pass Creek area. Larry dreamed of the day he could move there and raise chickens.

We bought a little old trailer which we put on the property, and we built an outhouse and a shed and began spending long weekends there. Larry ran the business with the cell phone, and we were able to relax a little. We loved having bonfires and wiener roasts with our family there, and it was wonderful to get away once in a while.

When we were home in Abbotsford, during the week, I drove into New Westminster to spend the day with Mom. We would go to a restaurant of her choice for lunch; and then we would buy her groceries, take them up to her suite, and put them away before I headed home. Although our children were busy and lived in different cities, we tried to have time together with them too.

In 1993 a lady from our church told me about a Bible study she was attending which sounded interesting. I had read through the Bible but did not know how to study it, and this study by Kay Arthur was what I needed. I began going to the studies, and that was the beginning of a long-term relationship with Precept Bible Studies. The studies gave me a solid foundation in the Word of God.

From then on I was involved in a Precept Bible Study every week at the Central Heights Mennonite Church, and we began attending there on Sunday mornings with our friends. Whenever possible I attended the annual seminars for Precept leaders and potential leaders that were held in the Lower Mainland area. I wanted to teach others.

Our business was thriving, and we prayed for more trucks and hired more people when the work was beyond what we could handle. When the deliveries were for customers who were out of town I would usually go with Larry, and we would stay in a motel overnight. We worked very well together. I was comfortable with computers, so I did the bookkeeping, and Larry knew the city, the drivers, and the dispatching, so he handled that end of the business usually with his cell phone.

In December 1996 we decided to drive to Castlegar to spend Christmas with Dwayne, Maureen, and our grandchildren, Ayron and Shawn. We didn't check the weather report as road conditions were never an issue if we decided to go somewhere. Driving to Castlegar was uneventful; the road was good, and we made excellent time.

While we were there we went out to our property to shovel the snow off the roof of our little old trailer. Two of the international college students living with Dwayne and Maureen went with us, and we all walked through waist-deep snow to reach the trailer. Larry was caught off guard when the snow slid off the roof, knocked him down the bank, and buried him under the avalanche. We were all concerned but managed to rescue him and pulled him to safety.

After a beautiful Christmas with everyone it was time to return home. Again we did not think to check the weather report. If we had we might not have gone that day, and we would have missed a great adventure. We wanted to be home before Monday, so at 8:00 AM on Sunday, December 29, we set out on the eight-hour drive through the mountains toward Abbotsford.

The roads were a little icy in places, and there was some drifting snow, but we made good time to Princeton which was about halfway. As we drove through the mountain passes between Princeton and Hope, we noticed that the snow was drifting more, and the road was treacherous in places, but Larry was not overly concerned; he had driven semi trucks on roads like that before.

Arriving at Chilliwack we found that the highways leaving there were closed, and all the motels and hotels we phoned were full. We decided we would drive to the Rainbow Country Inn, park outside, and stay in the car for the night. When we woke up the next morning we saw all kinds and sizes of cars and trucks around us.

Larry went in to the hotel and came back with coffee and news; volunteers would serve food at 7:00 AM. When we went in at 7:15 there were about one hundred people sleeping or milling around in the lobby plus a few dogs. We heard this was the worst storm in seventy-five years with winds 60 to 90 kilometers per hour and 30 centimeters of new snow expected that evening. Everyone was staying another night.

All roads were closed for two nights and three days, and finally on the third evening we ventured to leave on the #7 highway, the long way home. We counted our blessings as we were well taken care of with food in the hotel, a warm car to sleep in, and we got to know a lot of people we would not have met otherwise.

We were thankful for cell phones with which Larry was able to manage the dispatching and all the other business. Thankfully we arrived home safe and sound, and Larry had another story to add to his repertoire. The year 1996 ended on a high note, but the next year would prove to have many challenges.

Sadly in January 1997, Brenda and Adrian separated. As I lived some miles away from where Brenda was living with friends, I did not see her often. We did meet for lunch or dinner occasionally, and we spoke on the phone, so we kept in touch, but she wanted to live her life without any interference from us, and I respected her wishes. I was concerned, but I did not feel free to ask questions about her personal affairs.

When she phoned and said she had lost her job, she was vague about where she was staying, and we had no way to contact her as we didn't know her friends. My worst fears were realized when I found out she was on drugs. Even then she hid the facts from us as much as possible. Once, we helped her leave a dangerous situation she was living in, and another time we paid a drug debt because we were afraid of the consequences for her if it was not paid.

In May I went for a week of prayer counseling with Elijah House Counseling Center. This was an answer to a prayer two years earlier. I had issues from my childhood, mainly my dad's verbal abuse and the hurt and anger I still felt. I wanted to be rid of my past. Although I had thought I would deal with the sexual abuse by an uncle, I found I could not talk about it. However, through prayer counseling, I was able to be free of the emotional abuse of my dad.

During the week of counseling, our business was under attack. Our checks didn't come in, and our finances were held back. Three of our drivers had truck trouble, and one driver was in a car accident. Larry began having chest pains which concerned us because of a previous heart attack. We had one week of stress and frustration, but the Lord was there, and I felt wonderfully calm, not stressed or emotional. I had total inner peace which was unusual for me.

In September I began taking the Elijah House Prayer Counseling Course. It was no accident that I was taking the course at that time because so much of what I was learning was helping me with the things I was going through. One thing I learned that I wished I had known earlier was that adopted children are wounded in their spirit in the womb, and they come with feelings of rejection. I felt that I had failed as a mother by not being there for my daughter as much as I should have been and for not being the example that she needed me to be.

In our small groups we practiced what we were learning, and one night I was the counselee who presented my issue to the counselor, Dorothy. "I am torn between my husband and my daughter; her crisis has become my crisis. I think I am rescuing her, but Larry feels I am being sucked into the whirlpool of her financial dilemma."

Dorothy suggested that Larry and I work out a policy negotiating how far we can go financially and setting a time limit which I will tell Brenda about. That sounded like good advice. She prayed for each one of us specifically—a softened heart for Larry, a lack of fear for me, and divine appointments for Brenda.

The Holy Spirit is such a faithful teacher, and He had more to teach me about this. That night after the session, I sat in my car listening to some tapes by Jim Richards. He said we need to know what is our stuff and what is the other person's stuff. We don't want them to suffer the consequences, but when we keep them from the reaping, we short-circuit the process of God working in their life. My heart was breaking as I wept for her. I knew I had to let her go.

The father in the story Jesus told about the prodigal son must have had similar feelings as he gave him his inheritance and then let him go. He didn't know if he would ever see him again, and I didn't know what would become of my daughter. I tried to protect her when she was a child, now I could no longer do that. I felt her pain.

I had dreams that she was in danger, and once when I woke up about 2:00 AM praying for her, the Lord spoke to me and said, "You are trying to control everything again." I said I gave her to the Lord, but I was having a hard time letting go. In the past I had tried to control everything, and she didn't want me to control anything.

Over the next months I fasted and prayed many times to break the spiritual strongholds on Brenda. I contacted everyone I knew and every ministry I could think of asking them to pray for her. Twice I received a note from Samaritan's Purse saying they were praying for her. That touched me deeply.

The Lord impressed me with the need to travail in prayer. Like the birthing process, travailing in prayer is labor. I knew that intercession was the only answer. He was building in me a spirit of tenacity in prayer which I would need as I went through trials in the next years. God answered all of the prayer, especially the one Dorothy prayed for Brenda to have divine appointments.

As I was preparing to go out one morning, Brenda phoned. She wanted to know if I could arrange a ticket for her to leave the downtown core and go out to a friend's place in another city. I told her to call me back in ten minutes; I would have the answer. When she called back I had arranged a train ticket, and she was able to leave the city that day. She told us later about the incidents surrounding her decision to leave the street.

Like the prodigal son, she was barely surviving in the pig pen (skid row). The Lord used three people to cause her to leave the street. The sandwich lady, who came to the street every night with hot food, went to her and prayed that she would leave the street and not come back. The man at the needle exchange told her, "You don't belong here."

The next morning when she woke up, she told the girl sleeping on the cardboard next to her, "I don't belong here." The girl's response was "You finally saw it; call home." She knew she did not belong there, and all she needed was encouragement to call home. The next months were not easy as she struggled to overcome the addiction to drugs.

People at the Indian Friendship Center and the Union Gospel Mission were kind and understanding, and with counseling she was able to make a full recovery. On the downward path she had lost all her material possessions and even her health. Within a few months she had a job and eventually moved to another province where she felt she could make a fresh start. It was a long, long climb out, but she made it.

The evening of June 19, 1998, we wrapped up the Prayer Counseling Course with a time of fellowship. The leaders closed our time together with a word of prophecy over each person. Della spoke the Mary blessing over me saying that my desire to sit at the feet of Jesus, like Mary, brings joy to His heart. Brian spoke the Grandmother blessing over me saying that grandchildren, not my own, would see Jesus in me and feel secure while I was holding their hand.

For a number of years we talked to various people about our desire to sell the business. Two couples had come close to buying it, but for some reason it never happened. At sixty-seven years of age, Larry was getting tired of constantly working with very little time to rest. We did not know that Glen and Norine, Larry's brother and his wife, were considering buying the business.

Then one day Glen came to us and said they felt the Lord had told them to buy our business. They wanted the financial information to send to their accountant, and we would go from there. We were very excited because they would already know the drivers and many of our customers. They also had more expertise than we did because of their previous experience in the business world.

From the fall of 1998 to the spring of 1999, accountants and lawyers were busy as preparation was being made for the selling of our business and all that was involved to make that happen as smoothly as possible. As Glen's lawyer and accountant were in Edmonton and ours was in Abbotsford, it meant that there would also be traveling time. Everything was finalized just before the long weekend in May 1999.

We were very excited about taking our Fifth Wheel to Pass Creek and having a much needed holiday. We stayed overnight along the way and arrived at the property on Friday afternoon. Larry was having discomfort in his chest, so we decided to go and check it out at the Castlegar Hospital Emergency. After some tests the doctor said it was indigestion, and we could go home. Larry told me afterward that the discomfort was still there when we walked out of the hospital, but we went home believing the diagnosis of the doctor. That was a mistake that almost cost Larry his life.

Chapter 9
The Breakers

"All Your breakers and Your rolling waves have gone over me. Yet the Lord will command His loving-kindness in the daytime, and in the night His song shall be with me,"

—Psalm 42:7,8 (AMP)

The next morning Larry came into the cabin where I was working. He had been moving some downed trees out of the creek and was now in excruciating pain and sweating profusely. Immediately I phoned for an ambulance, hoping they would be able to find our place easily.

Within an hour the Ambulance had picked him up, and he was in the Castlegar hospital. This time all the tests showed that he had a major heart attack. The specialist who was brought from Nelson requested that he be transferred to the Nelson hospital. Our four children who all lived in other places came and stayed with Dwayne and Maureen.

The calls went out to family and friends, to churches and prayer groups to pray for Larry. On Tuesday, June 1, Larry was flown by Air Ambulance to Vancouver, and Dwayne and I set out by car so we could be there when he came out of surgery. Over the next two days he had angioplasty surgery with four stents put in, and by Sunday he was scheduled to come home, but that did not happen.

When I arrived at his room to take him home, the curtain was pulled around his bed, and I saw feet under the curtain. The nurse stopped me and asked me to wait for the doctor in the family room. When he came, he said that Larry had a setback but was fine now. Larry told me later that he had a cardiac arrest that morning, and they had used the paddles three times before his heart started up.

He was moved to another room and stayed there until Saturday when he was allowed to go home to Abbotsford. Within the week Larry was in the intensive care of the Abbotsford hospital. When our doctor received the medical reports on Larry, he called him a "miracle man." He was in four hospitals in one month.

Through it all we had a peace that passes understanding. One night while I was driving to the hospital, I found myself singing Psalm 91:1-2 over and over: "He that dwelleth in the secret place of the Most High shall abide under the shadow of the Almighty. I will say of the Lord, He is my refuge and my fortress, my God, in Him will I trust."

When we listed our condo in Abbotsford for sale, we were told by the real estate agent that there were over three hundred condos for sale in the area "so don't count on it selling anytime soon." But they reckoned without God. A week after we went back to Pass Creek to finish our holiday, the agent phoned us that he had a buyer. We had planned to spend summers at Pass Creek and winters in Abbotsford, but it was not to be that way. Suddenly we needed a house on our property.

In the past we had looked at manufactured homes, and we had some idea of the plan we liked. We found one in Castlegar that was right for us. After it was delivered and set up, we drove back to Abbotsford to pack and move. Soon the papers were signed, the condo was sold, and we could settle down to the quieter life in the beautiful Pass Creek area.

We were so thankful for the family and friends who helped us with the move, those who helped us move from Abbotsford, and those who were waiting at our property to move us in. They'll never know what it meant to us. We were tired from everything we had been through, and their willingness to help warmed our hearts.

The cabin with its windows facing the creek became my office, and I spent many hours there studying for the Bible studies I planned to teach in January. We had a very nice deck built on the side of our home that faced the creek. Larry got the chickens he wanted, and he had regular customers who bought the eggs. He planted a garden with a fence around it to keep the wild animals out of it.

Our country life was completed with a five-year-old dog named Prince from the animal shelter and a calico kitten we named Cali. Prince helped Larry keep the bears under control and was his constant companion wherever he went. We had wiener roasts with family and friends, and we were making new friends in the church we attended.

The pastor asked me to be part of the Small Group's leadership and possibly lead a group in the Pass Creek area. We were glad to close the book on 1999 with its many twists and turns, and we looked forward to a quiet life—the two of us in our home by the creek. Fear dominated media attention to the year 2000 as possible catastrophes were predicted. People were advised to expect computer problems.

The year 2000 dawned with hardly a ripple. All the presupposed catastrophes with computers never materialized on the scale they expected, and the world seemed to be ticking along fine. I was preparing to lead my first Bible study in this area with three other ladies in Esther's kitchen, listening to Kay Arthur's teaching.

On the morning of January 18, I had gone to the cabin for my usual quiet time and was just coming back to the house when Larry met me with the phone in his hand. He said Dwayne was on the phone, but he couldn't understand what he was saying; it was something about Shawn. Dwayne was not on the phone, and no one answered the home phone, so we decided to drive in to town to the hospital.

When we walked into the family room the first person I saw was Maureen, and she said, "There's no hope." Larry put his arms around Dwayne and Maureen, and we all just cried together. They said Shawn was in the emergency, and the doctors were working on him, but it did not look good. Someone said, "The nurse suggested if someone was religious we should pray." We put our arms around Dwayne and Maureen and prayed for a miracle, but the miracle didn't happen.

I could not reach our pastor, so I called retired Pastor Ira Johnson. He had married Dwayne and Maureen twenty years before, and now he and Adeline were there to help in a time of crisis. Without hesitation they came to the hospital to be with us, sharing our grief and loss. The scripture on my calendar had read, "Peace I leave with you, My peace I give you, do not be afraid." Lord, I need Your peace now!

That night when we got home, I got out one of the tapes for the Bible study we were going to do on the names of God. As I listened to "Run Into His arms, He's El Shaddai," I found comfort from my Father. He had chosen not to give Shawn back to us.

I don't understand, but I accept that He knows best. Many times I had prayed for Shawn to be kept from the evils of this world. Was this the answer? And the prayer that Shawn would be used mightily for God was that answered by his death which had impacted so many young people, especially his classmates.

Apparently seventeen-year-old Shawn was in his drama class at school when suddenly, without a word, he slipped from the chair to the floor. That day his mom, an educational assistant, was working in the high school, and she was called to that room to resuscitate a student which turned out to be her own son.

She and another teacher administered CPR, working on him until the ambulance arrived. The paramedics did what they could and then transported him to the hospital emergency where for the next hour the doctors did everything possible, but he could not be revived. An autopsy later revealed he had Uhl's disease.

The next few days were busy as relatives and friends from far and near began arriving. There was an overwhelming response from coworkers, friends, and people from the community as they came to express their sympathy and support. Dwayne and Maureen have both lived here for most of their lives, and they are known and respected by many people in the community.

A memorial held at the high school was attended by over one thousand students, faculty, and parents, and a funeral service at the church was filled to capacity with people even standing outside. Our children were all there as well as some of the international college students who had lived in Dwayne and Maureen's home and been part of their children's lives through the years.

We were reminded again of how special Shawn was and how his life touched so many people. His vivid imagination and his sense of humor amused everyone. One camping trip he and his dad were throwing peanuts to the squirrels and gradually dropping the peanuts closer to their chairs. Shawn got an idea. He tied dental floss around a peanut and threw the peanut down.

A squirrel grabbed the peanut, took off, reached the end of the string, did a flip backward, lost the peanut, recovered, and went for the peanut again. This time it did not run with it, so Shawn, holding the end of the dental floss, got up from his chair, and the squirrel walked off with the peanut in his mouth. Shawn walked along behind the squirrel through the campsite like he was walking his dog.

He was so happy when he grew to over six feet tall and was finally taller than his sister, Ayron. Standing beside her and looking down on her he would bring it to everyone's attention. Of course we laughed with them, knowing how really important this was to him.

Larry asked the big question, "Why did God spare me and not him? Why did I live through a major heart attack and cardiac arrest, and Shawn, at seventeen years old, have heart failure and not live?" I have heard it said, "When you lose a parent you lose your past; when you lose a spouse, you lose the present, and when you lose a child you lose your future." We lost a part of our future, the only son of my only son!

Yes, we grieve our loss but not as those without hope. We have an underlying peace in the midst of our tears that shows God's enabling power in us. "We have this treasure in earthen vessels, to show that the transcendent power belongs to God and not to us." I relinquish all the hopes I had for Shawn into the keeping of my Father Who alone knows and does all things well.

A few nights later, Larry was having chest pains, and we called the ambulance. He was taken to the Trail hospital where he stayed until he was flown to Vancouver for an angiogram. This time he did not need any more angioplasty for which he was thankful. He visited family while he was in that area and flew home on February 7, tired and happy to be home again with his wife and his chickens.

On WMC Sunday I gave my testimony at church. I compared the parable of the sower and seed to my growth in the things of God. I mentioned times in my life when I had heard and responded to the Word of God which was planted in my heart. One young man said that he understood the gospel for the first time in his life, and he opened his heart to it. A short time after that I gave my testimony at a Women's Aglow meeting, speaking about Christ being my anchor.

One Sunday morning I went to the altar for prayer for healing, and after the pastor anointed me with oil and prayed for me, he prophesied over me and confirmed the call on my life. He said, "God is revealing Himself and what his purpose for your life is. This mandate is not new to you, you have known this. It will not be easy." Although I do know this, I don't understand it. It will need to be a work of God totally.

We began our Bible study with much enthusiasm. The other ladies had never been involved in a study that used material and tapes from the Precept ministries. Although we were using cassette tapes and not videos, our desire to know the Word of God was strong, and that brought us together every week. As we learned about the character and the faithfulness of God, our faith in Him grew.

The next year we enjoyed Kay's teaching by video in the church where more people were able to participate in the studies with us. For the next eight years I taught Bible studies, and those who took part in them seemed to enjoy them. It was not always the same people who came, but there were a faithful few who stayed with it year after year, always ready to study and grow in their knowledge of God's Word.

In 2004 I had knee replacement surgery. Although it was a very painful procedure I am thankful for it now as I can walk better, and even stairs are no longer a problem. The day of my surgery, Larry had fallen at home and injured his knees. When Dwayne and Maureen brought him to visit me in the hospital, he was in a wheelchair. I teased him that he was trying to upstage me.

For the next four years I was very involved in our little church. The bookkeeper could no longer do the books, so I took over that. A number of people had left, and we found ourselves in redevelopment mode. I was asked to be part of the leadership committee, and I was still teaching a morning and an evening Bible study. Larry always went with me to the studies. We both enjoyed them.

One summer the kids decided to have a family campout down near the creek. Dwayne and Maureen stayed for the weekend with their truck and camper, and Brenda and Kirk and their family had tents. There was even a place where they could swim further up the road. Another summer Gayle and Steven came up from Arizona, and Ryan, Wendy, and children came from Calgary to get together and visit us.

Occasionally we talked about selling our property and moving into town. Although we liked the quiet life, there were drawbacks to living there. The winter's snow on the roof of our home and on the winding mountain roads we traveled was a concern. Larry had fewer chickens now, but they still needed to be tended to, and he was getting tired. He didn't always feel well.

So one day in March 2007, we contacted a realtor; they came out to our property, and before long we had a deal. The property was sold with a closing date of June 1, 2007. Years before this Dwayne and Maureen had told us that when the time came their basement suite would be ready for us to move into. I phoned them to see if it would be available, and Dwayne assured me that it would be.

With the stress of packing and moving I lost forty pounds which was a good thing. Besides the health benefit I was able to give away old clothes and invest in a new wardrobe. Our move was made easier because of all the help we had. The pastor, youth, and some people from the church, as well as Dwayne, Maureen, other family members and friends were all on hand to help us

After we settled into our new home we gave our Taurus to the new pastor, and we bought a new 2008 Toyota. We wanted to do some traveling. Previously we had always found it difficult to go away together for any length of time because of having animals to look after, so now we would be able to enjoy a holiday together.

The first significant event after our move was in April 2008 when I had angioplasty surgery in the Royal Columbian hospital. I did not stay in the hospital overnight as Dustin, a perfusionist, was able to look after me at home. We had some excitement when the wound needed stitching, and I went by ambulance to the White Rock hospital in the night.

Sadly, for us, the next event was when my mom had a heart attack and went to be with her Lord on June 6. She was ninety-three years old. We drove to the Coast and stayed with Dustin and Laura Lee. As her executor I took care of her business affairs, and Eleanor and I cleaned out her apartment. At the celebration of her life, Dwayne read her eulogy, and other grandchildren read stories of her life and songs she had written.

She was the Proverbs 31 woman, "She looked well to the ways of her household and did not eat the bread of idleness. Her children rise up and call her blessed."

Chapter 10
The Depths Of The Sea Made A Way

"Was it not You Who dried up the Red Sea, the waters of the great deep, Who made the depths of the sea a way for the redeemed to pass over?"

—Isaiah 51:10 (AMP)

In September we took the trip we had talked about for a long time to the Peace River country in Alberta. Although Larry and I had lived there in 1959 in different circumstances, the memories of our time there revolved around the same people with similar experiences. We stayed with Joyce, my former sister-in-law, who was, as only she can be, the most caring hostess, and we had a good visit with our friends Dollye and Basil, reminiscing about old times.

On our way to the Peace, we spent a couple of days visiting with Brenda in Edmonton. She gave us a tour of where she works and the big truck she drives. Larry, being a trucker, was very impressed that our daughter could drive a truck like that. A month after we got home, on October 22, Brenda presented us with our grandson, Joshua James. In December, she and Josh flew to Castlegar to visit us.

On March 4, 2009, my sister's husband, Vern, died suddenly. They did not know he had cancer until it was too late. This was especially hard for Eleanor as it was only nine months since our mother's passing. We drove down to be with the family. Twelve-year-old Bailey sang and played his guitar at his grandpa's funeral. He did very well, and his grandpa would have been so proud of him.

In the fall, Eleanor came to visit us for a couple of weeks. As she had never spent time here before, we had the pleasure of driving her around the area, showing her our beautiful scenery. We enjoyed being together, reconnecting after not seeing each other much in the intervening years. With our quiet lifestyle, she said she experienced a peace after the previous ordeal of losing her husband so suddenly.

The next May, Larry decided to go hunting with his brothers, so we drove to the Coast. Herb and Doreen were waiting for us in Chilliwack, Larry went with them, and I drove on to Langley to spend the time with Eleanor. This was like the country mouse visiting the city mouse because there is so much to do where she lives, and I like shopping and eating in restaurants that we don't have in our area.

When the hunting trip was over, Larry and I spent a few days with Dustin, Laurie, and Elizabeth; and on our way home we stayed overnight with Brenda and Kirk. Although Larry enjoyed being with his brothers, some things about his trip had been disappointing; he had not taken enough clothes, and he was cold at night when he went to bed. When we came home, Larry was sick and had to take antibiotics.

After that trip, Larry's health seemed to deteriorate even more. He kept saying, "Something's wrong. I don't know what it is, but I know something is wrong." He was deathly afraid he was getting Alzheimer's. Because of all they went through with Ida when she had Alzheimer's, it was his greatest fear. He got extremely upset with me once when I tried to play down the Alzheimer angle. He apologized after and then said, "See, this is what can happen."

We went to our family doctor who could find nothing wrong. One afternoon we went to emergency, and the doctor on call was the one who had misdiagnosed him the night he was having his heart attack. He had always remembered us, and when he saw Larry, he said, "Oh, no!" We all laughed. He could find nothing wrong, but as a result of that visit, Larry was sent for every test imaginable, one being a CT scan.

The tests did not reveal anything out of the ordinary, but Larry did not feel well, and his next fear surfaced. He was afraid he would end up as a burden to me which was something he did not want to happen. I could not relieve his fears, and he did not appreciate me trying.

We attended church each week, but Larry did not enjoy the social aspect of it like he used to. Most of the time we didn't stay for the community lunch which was a part of the fellowship after the Sunday service. Often we met Dwayne and Maureen for lunch at a restaurant instead, and we enjoyed that. If they couldn't meet us, then the two of us would go out to a restaurant instead of the church lunch.

In December we drove to the Coast to have Christmas with Dustin, Laura Lee, and Elizabeth. We rented the guest suite for the week and had a very nice holiday. We had a beautiful Christmas with our family. We also took time to meet with friends, Marge and Earle and Verna and Jim. On our way home we stayed in Chilliwack and met Larry's brother, Herb, and his wife, Doreen, for supper in a restaurant. So we had a good time with people we love and enjoy being with.

On May 27, 2010, I attended a seminar on grief with Alan Wolfelt. It was held in the Sandman with about two hundred people attending. It was interesting and informative. As a result of the seminar, I contacted the funeral home about preplanned funerals, and a gentleman came a week later and set that up for Larry and me.

In November of that year, Larry's two daughters, Gayle and Brenda, came for a brief visit. It was good to see them, and Larry really enjoyed their time here. He was able to reminisce with them about their past history that I was not a part of but which he needed to talk about.

We had Christmas with Dwayne, Maureen, and Ayron and Stefan who came home to spend Christmas with Ayron's parents this year. It was nice to be together for Christmas Eve and breakfast. By lunch time I was sick, and one by one everyone in the house came down with the flu. I was not able to even eat Christmas dinner because of it.

So now we have come back to where we began this journey. I was packing my books in February, planning to move away from Castlegar back to the big city. Although it is not quite a year since Larry passed, it seems so much longer than that. I'll always be glad I had the privilege of being his wife; he was a man of integrity, and he loved the Lord with all his heart. In memory I hear him praying for each member of the family in the morning when he gets up and at night after he is in bed.

Missing You

Alone, at the top of the stairs I stand,
I miss the touch of your comforting hand.
You're gone, we never said good-bye.
For that, in silence, I can only cry.

Your chair is where you waited for me,
To join you with our afternoon tea.
But you're not there; you will never be again.
My heart remembers with sadness and pain.

There we laughed and often talked too,
Expressing our different points of view.
We reminisced of memories past,
Twenty-seven years went by so fast.

You came so close one time before
But God kindly gave us ten years more.
You're taken now; God called you again,
To a better place that is free from pain.

A part of me left too, on that day
My life is ordered now a different way.
Alone, yet not alone, I know,
I feel God's leading as I onward go.

My faith in God and His sure plan for me
Will guide me on, until your face I see.
We'll meet again on heaven's shore
And then I know we'll part no more.

Until then, remember, what we often said, "I love you!"
And the reply as always was, "I love you more!"

Epilogue

Alone, Growing In Grace

"Even to your old age I am He, and even to hair white with age
will I carry you. I have made, and I will bear; yes, I will carry
and will save you."

—Isaiah 46:4 (AMP)

By the time this is published, I will have been alone one year. After twenty-seven years of companionship, I am slowly adjusting to going everywhere alone. Although we have had sadness, within this year we also have great gladness in the birth of my first great-grandson, Madden Shawn Tomas, born to Ayron and Stefan.

Looking back on my life, I thank God for Larry and his unconditional love. He told me often that he loved me and that I made a difference in his life. When he told me I was beautiful, it made me feel beautiful in spite of what I look like on the outside. My heart opened up as I felt valued and wanted by another human being.

We were good for each other as we could talk about anything and everything. In the beginning of our relationship we talked for hours. We shared our hopes and dreams and treasured the time we could spend together, counting the hours apart as meaningless until we could meet again. We knew real communication on many levels.

I grew more, spiritually and emotionally, when I was free to grow; and Larry encouraged me to be the best I could be. I could never have learned to love and be loved if he and I had not got together. Even the problems we encountered were a growing and learning time for us.

J. Vernon McGee's counsel to young people about to be married was this: Marriage is made on three different planes. The first is the physical plane, the sexual relationship which is important. The second plane in a marriage is the mental or psychological relationship which is also very important. When a husband and wife have similar interests and enjoy doing things together, it makes for a healthy relationship.

The third plane in a marriage is the spiritual relationship which is vitally important. A husband and wife should be able to pray and meet around the Word of God together. Ecclesiastes 4:12 says, "A threefold cord is not quickly broken." Larry and I met on all three planes.

After reading McGee's premarriage counseling advice, I know my first marriage failed because it was broken on two planes; we didn't have similar interests, and we were never on the same plane spiritually, although I had thought we were before we were married.

The positives that came out of that marriage exceed the negatives as I look at my children who somehow, in spite of what was missing in the home they grew up in, have become loving human beings, raising their own children with patience and wisdom.

I regret that I was unable to encourage my children to reach for the stars. I know they had the ability and the intelligence to be anything they set their minds to, but I never told them that. I could not rise above my own feelings of inadequacy as a mother and as a person.

Paula Sandford, in *Healing Women's Emotions*, says, "It is not our job to redeem the mistakes we have made with our children, that is the Lord's job." I know the Lord will redeem the mistakes I made. They were dedicated to Him, and they belong to Him. "I know Whom I have believed and am persuaded that He is able to keep that which I've committed to Him against that day" (2 Tim. 1:12).

I thank God for blessing me with my son, Dwayne, of whom I am so proud. I was privileged as his mom to watch him grow up and become a man who is caring and considerate, a loving husband and father. I'm thankful for Maureen, his wife, who has been more than a daughter-in-law; she's been a caring daughter to me as she and Dwayne have walked with me through some of the valleys.

I thank God for bringing Brenda, my beautiful daughter, into my life. I had the privilege of being her mom and watching her grow into a loving, caring woman of courage and determination. We lived through some of the difficult years together, sometimes with laughter and other times with tears. Even now her phone calls encourage me.

I'm grateful for my grandchildren, Ayron (Stefan) and Joshua (Brenda's son), and now my great-grandchild, Madden. God's blessings truly extend to all generations.

I'm also thankful for my stepchildren, Gayle, Brenda D., and Dustin and their children and grandchildren. When Larry and I married, we became a blended family; and he made a point of claiming all the children as "ours," allowing no distinctions as in yours and mine. He loved my children, and they loved him. Our children were all adults when we got together, and they get along well with each other.

Although I have a good relationship with Gayle and Brenda, I have a closer relationship with Dustin and his wife, Laura Lee. From the beginning, they called me Mom, and even now they keep in contact with me the most often. To their daughter, Elizabeth, I have always been Nana. On my birthday last year, Elizabeth insisted on taking me out for dinner to the Olive Garden. We have an important bond.

In 1984, Larry had only three grandchildren, Ryan and Christy (Gayle's) and Nathan (Brenda and Kirk's). Five more were born after we got together. Nathan was two years old, and I was "Auntie Janna" to him then. When Larry and I went to their place, Nathan would want me to read his books with him. As the years have gone by, the children are grown up with their own families now, and our contact is limited.

Brenda and Kirk's son, Ben, played the piano and sang a special song that he had composed for Larry's Memorial in Castlegar, which I really appreciated. He has a prophetic gift and recently sent me a word of prophecy which the Lord had given him for me. I had been having some "down" times, and the word he gave me was so encouraging. His obedience to the Lord blessed me greatly.

Right now, I am teaching a Bible study which I love to do. Once more it's a study by Kay Arthur, this time on the book of 1 Peter. I still feel useful; I am not without promise as Psalm 92:14-15 says, "(Growing in grace) they shall still bring forth fruit in old age; they are living memorials to show that the Lord is faithful." There has always been fruit from the studies we have done in the past. Former students will confirm this. They love these studies as much as I do.

I'm also writing books and having them published. This is my third book which has taken some months to complete. Writing about my life has been a soul-searching experience with laughter and tears as I have relived the past. I want to live my life to the full, enjoying every day as it comes so that when I leave this earth my purpose for being here has been accomplished and I will hear my Savior say, "Well done, good and faithful servant."

I close with an encouraging word which I pray will be true for you. "When you come to the edge of all you know to do and you step over, you will find God's hands underneath you, or He will give you wings."

Pictures

Ayron

Brenda

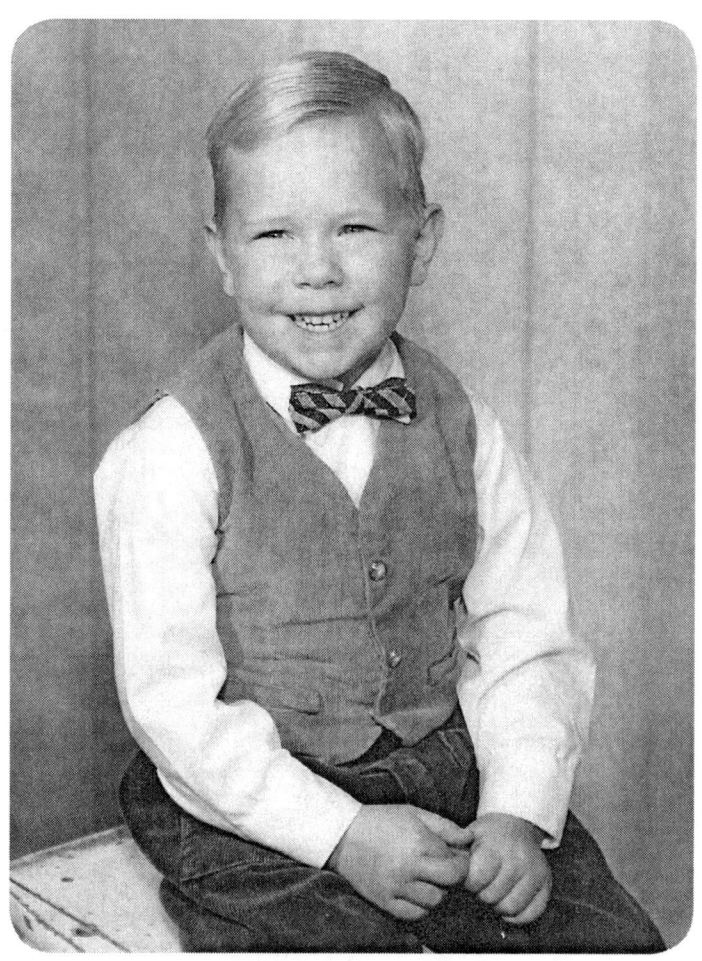

Dwayne

Dwayne, Maureen, Ayron, Shawn

Elizabeth

Eva and Otto Olsen wedding—0099

Grandma & Grandpa Olsen

Josh

Larry and I

Larry, Jeff, Dustin (3 generations)

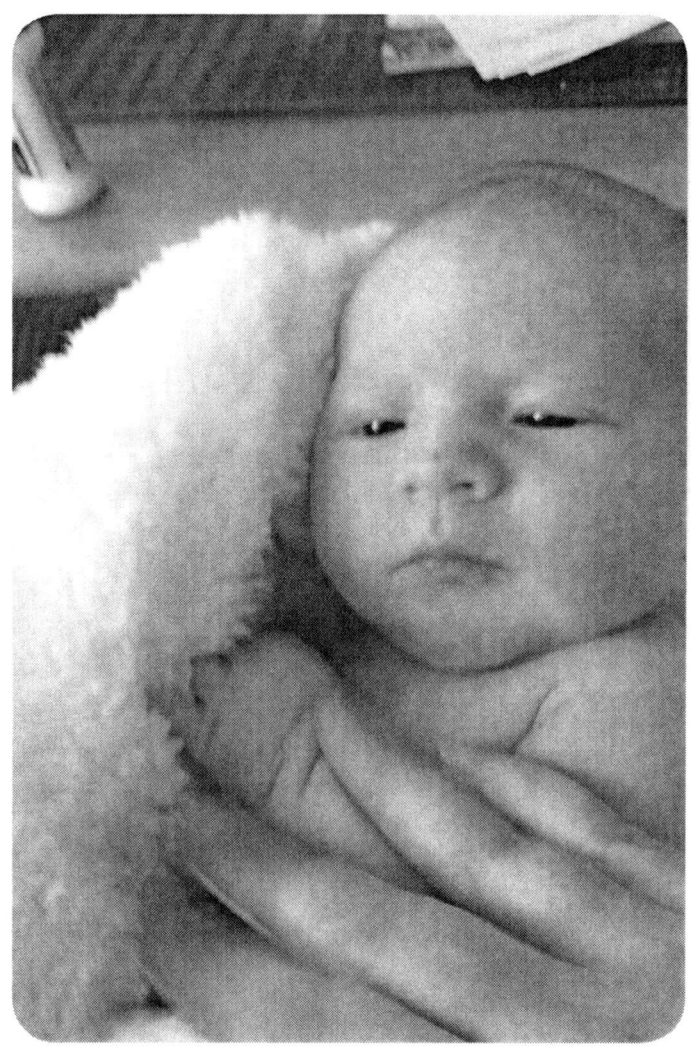

Madden

Me at 3 or 4 years old

Mom and three children 1940's—0067

My brother, sister and me

Nana & Grandpa Phillips

Nana Phillips

Ole & Janna Olsen, family of Otto as a child

Orv, Mom, Eleanor, me

Shawn 17 years old

Tom & Alice Phillips, family of Eva as child

Brenda, grad

Appendix A

Explanation of Terms: Saved, Salvation, Accept Jesus as Savior

These are all Bible words meaning the same thing. In the beginning of time, God created man with the purpose of having fellowship with Him, but the first created human beings, Adam and Eve, rebelled against God and followed their own desires. This sin was punishable by death, both physical and spiritual death, separation from God forever.

Everyone born from then on was born in sin and under the penalty of death (Romans 5:12). God had a plan in place before the foundation of the world that would bring man back into fellowship. The penalty of death could be paid by one perfect, sinless man as a substitute for all mankind. That One was Jesus, the sinless Son of God, Who came to earth, was born of a virgin, lived as a man, died as a man, shed His blood for us, rose from the dead, and now lives and intercedes for us.

Jesus Christ died for all, but all are not automatically free from the penalty of death. Each person must believe that His death was in their place, an effective substitute for their sin, and they must accept His Lordship over their life and follow Him. They are then saved.

The ABC of Salvation

A—ADMIT that you are a sinner in need of a Savior. Romans 3:23: "All have sinned." You cannot do enough good works to pay the penalty.

Ephesians 2:8-9: "Not of works, lest any man should boast."

95

B—BELIEVE that Jesus Christ paid the penalty in full for your sins.

1 Corinthians 15:1-3: "Christ died for our sins according to the Scriptures."

Acts 16:31: "Believe on the Lord Jesus Christ and you shall be saved."

John 6:28,29: The Jews asked Jesus, "What are we to do to carry out what God requires?" Jesus replied, "This is the work (service) that God asks of you, that you believe in the One Whom He has sent."

C—COMMIT your life to Him by telling Him, "Jesus, I believe You died in my place, and I accept You now as my Lord and Savior. Thank You for saving me. I commit my life to you."

Appendix B

Explanation of Terms: Tongues, Baptism of Holy Spirit

The book of Acts begins with Jesus giving the apostles instructions before He leaves them. He commands them to wait in Jerusalem for the promised baptism of the Holy Spirit which they will receive. Jesus goes back to heaven; and about one hundred and twenty people, including Mary, the mother of Jesus, his brothers, and the apostles follow His instructions and gather in an upper room in Jerusalem to wait.

Acts 2:1-4 says that on the day of Pentecost, there was a noise of rushing wind and tongues as of fire rested on each one of them, and "they were all filled with the Holy Spirit and began to speak with other tongues." Other people heard the tongues as in languages that they recognized. Peter preached; three thousand people repented, were baptized in Jesus' Name, and also received the gift of the Holy Spirit. This was where and when the baptism of the Holy Spirit began.

Peter says (2:39), "The promise is for you, your children and for all who are far off, as many as the Lord our God shall call to Himself." In Acts 10, Peter is asked to go to speak to Gentiles (non-Jews), and as he is telling them about Jesus, the Holy Spirit comes upon them, and they also speak in tongues and are then baptized in water in Jesus' Name.

Today, there are many people all over the world who are baptized in the Holy Spirit, and they speak in tongues. This experience is sometimes referred to as Pentecostal or Charismatic, but it is not limited to any one denomination nor is it limited to Protestants. The Holy Spirit also visited the Catholics with the result of new Charismatic communities forming.

Companions of the Cross was founded by Fr. Bob Bedard in 1985 and is still going today, although he passed away in 2011.

Although the baptism of the Holy Spirit and speaking in tongues is not accepted in all Christian circles, it is an experience that is very real and is not denied to the genuine seeker. Anyone who believes in Jesus Christ as their Savior may have this experience.

Some excellent books on the Holy Spirit I recommend are the following:

1. *An Eyewitness Remembers the Century of the Holy Spirit* by Vinson Synan, Chosen Books, 2010 Source: http://www.amazon.com/Eyewitness-Remembers-Century-Holy-Spirit/dp/0800794850
2. *In God's Providence: The Story of a Parish Coming Alive in the Holy Spirit* by Fr. John Randall, Koinonia Enterprises, May 1996
3. *Give God Permission: The Memoirs of Fr. Bob Bedard*, CC 2010 *www.companionscross.org*

Explanation of Prayer for Healing

When Jesus was on earth, He healed many people of various diseases. In Mark 16:14-20, we have the record of Jesus suddenly showing up where the eleven disciples were eating. After chiding them for their unbelief, He then sent them into the world to preach the gospel and perform miracles in His name. One miracle would be that when they prayed for the sick they would recover. The book of Acts records various kinds of healings by the disciples.

In James 5:14-15, we are given a pattern which is commonly used in various denominations. Many churches practice anointing with oil and praying over or with someone who requests special prayer for healing. The scripture says, "The prayer offered in faith will restore the one who is sick, and the Lord will raise him up." Faith is a prerequisite!

There have also been many evangelists with healing ministries who have held large crusades where the gift of healing was evident, and people were miraculously healed as a result. Some past ministers were Kathryn Kuhlman, Oral Roberts, John G. Lake, and Charles and Frances Hunter.

Hebrews 11:6 says, "And without faith it is impossible to please Him (God) for he who comes to God must believe that He is and that He is a rewarder of those who seek Him." Believe, ask, and receive.

Explanation of Falling When Meeting the Power of God

In Acts 9:3,4 "Now as he (Saul) traveled on, he came near to Damascus, and suddenly a light from heaven flashed around him. And he fell to the ground. Then he heard a voice saying to him, "Saul, Saul, why are you persecuting Me. And Saul said, "Who are You, Lord?" and He said, "I am Jesus, Whom you are persecuting."

Recounting this incident later before Agrippa, in Acts 26:14 "And when we had all fallen to the ground, I heard a voice in the Hebrew tongue saying to me, "Saul, Saul, why do you continue to persecute Me?"

God's power is not something we can stand up to.

Index

A

Adrian (Janna's son-in-law), 63, 68
Arthur, Kay, 65, 77, 93
Aspin, Shirley, 41
Ayron (Janna's granddaughter), 16, 52-53, 79, 90

B

Brenda (Janna's daughter), 46-49, 63, 68, 71, 84-85, 93
Brenda D. (Larry's daughter), 12

D

Dallas (Janna's first husband), 37-38, 40-44, 47-50, 53
Dorothy (Janna's counselor), 69-70
Dustin (Larry's son), 7, 11-12, 14, 83, 85-86, 92-93
Dwayne (Janna's son), 7, 14-15, 40-41, 43-49, 77-79, 81

E

Eleanor (Janna's sister), 21, 40, 83, 85
Elizabeth (Larry's granddaughter), 14, 26, 85-86, 93
explanation of
baptism of the Holy Spirit, 98
falling when meeting the power of God, 100
prayer for healing, 99 salvation, 96

G

Gayle (Larry's daughter), 13, 82, 87, 92-93
Geraldine (Janna's friend), 31
Glenn (Larry's brother), 16
Grandpa Phillips (Janna's grandfather), 20, 26

H

Healing Women's Emotions (Sandford), 92

101

CPSIA information can be obtained at www.ICGtesting.com
Printed in the USA
LVOW120624121212

311190LV00003B/19/P